THE GOD

CONCLUSION:

THE START OF A NEW BEGINNING

by ANNE RODGERS

THE GOD CONCLUSION

First Published by SHEARING
in 2011

Copyright © Anne Rodgers 2011

www.thegodconclusion.co.uk

ISBN 978-0-9569006-0-9

Printed and bound in Wales
by
I G PrintUK

ACKNOWLEDGEMENTS

A heartfelt thank you to the people who have given their time and understanding in helping me to make this book a reality. All the staff in my salon for their patience in the early days, and my niece Helen Hooper (little did she know just how much time was needed to understand my writing) who gave the book the start it needed. Victoria Green who helped put the book into context with much effort and hard work and Sally for reading it in its draft form. Chris, a long standing friend who has been a tower of strength when I could have easily given up and Mandy James whose sense of humour encouraged me to keep going. My sisters Janet, Dianne and Michelle who often checked my sanity and made sure I was still compos mentis in the early days. Also many thanks for all their support to my two sons Sean and Mark, my daughter Lucy and their families, Shirley McKay, Sharon Griffiths, Sally and Colin Dowd and to all my clients without whom this book would not have been possible.

CONTENTS

INTRODUCTION

For me, healing was the start of a new way of being.

My life today is completely different from the days when I owned a hairdressing salon. Being a hairdresser was all I had ever wanted; it fulfilled my dreams and suited me well. My salon was successful, I employed a talented team of stylists and together we had established a loyal clientele. I met all sorts of people from all walks of life and I am glad to have met each and every one of them. After thirty years of enjoying this wonderful work, I never thought that I would do anything different - but I could not have foreseen the dramatic event that would forever change my life.

The significance of that first night was not immediately apparent. It only began to make sense in the following months, after a series of events so incredible that in the beginning I could not even believe them myself. It was only when I could no longer refute the massive changes I was making to the lives of those around me that I began to really accept the new path upon which I had unwittingly found myself.

The events in which I have been involved and the things that I have been shown defy reality, or at least reality as I used to know it. In the course of my work as a healer, I have come to realise that much of what we take for granted, we have never truly examined. Many of our beliefs and values are passed on to us as social norms and family traditions, while others are acquired from religions, governments and even advertisements. And although some are certainly justified, too often we simply do not question why we believe what we believe.

The events of the past fifteen years have shaken my perception of reality to its very core. I have been challenged to honestly identify what I knew through my experiences to be real and to question what I assumed to be real because it was the way I expected it to be. In the beginning, that internal struggle wrestled with me constantly and even forced me to doubt my own sanity.

Thankfully, almost every single phenomenon has been witnessed by someone else. In the early days, I needed that reassurance - and to some extent still do - to give me the affirmation that comes from someone else witnessing what has taken place.

Those witnesses have included my friends and family, as well as clients and staff at my salon. Together we have felt the shock and disbelief that inevitably results from experiencing my gift - but the mistrust quickly wears off once people decide to accept what they can see, rather than believing what they think they are supposed to see.

I am very conscious of the struggle to accept what is not normally accepted and so I have hesitated until now to publish my experiences. While I have always kept a personal journal, resulting in thousands of pages of amazing accounts, I was unsure how effective these accounts would be without the reader being able to experience my work firsthand. I feared that what I had to share was just too bizarre for mainstream society to take seriously. But the thought of how many people I could potentially help if they only knew has continually nagged at me and so I am compelled to share my experiences. I do so in the belief that having knowledge of these true events which have changed so many lives may benefit others and bring hope and inspiration.

CHAPTER ONE – The Presence

September 1995

I was woken in the early hours of Tuesday 19th September by a whooshing sound. At first I just lay there, in that fuzzy state between sleep and consciousness. I listened, with my eyes closed, until I started to see a pale light. Startled, I opened my eyes, half expecting to see someone standing in my bedroom, but the room was empty and apart from the pale light, everything seemed as it should be. As my eyes focused, I saw pale lights on my ceiling. I lay there, mesmerised, as the ceiling began to spin, as though someone was slowly turning an umbrella. I thought I might be dreaming, but as I sat up in bed, I knew I was wide awake. I watched in awe as the ceiling span into a swirl of colour, slowly at first but as I watched the movement picked up speed and the whooshing sound became much louder and faster.

Questions began racing through my mind: 'What time is it? Why aren't I running out the door? How much faster and stronger is this going to get? Why am I not afraid?' I felt shock and disbelief rather than fear and I could not pull myself away.

My bedroom was pitch black except for the lights which were radiating from the ceiling to such an extent that the shape had almost entirely disappeared; it looked as though my ceiling had opened up. The spinning and the sound continued to grow and it didn't seem that it would stop anytime soon. I wanted to call my daughter Lucy into my room but I didn't, as I knew it would have frightened her. I didn't understand why no one else could hear the loud whooshing.

An urge came over me to get up onto my knees and move to the centre of the bed. But I hesitated as the force was so strong and loud and the energy from the spinning was throwing me off balance. By this time it had almost entirely encompassed my room. Finally on my knees, I felt an upsurge inside me like bubbles rising from fizzy pop, as if I was moving upwards and would soon become part of this colourful display. Then all around me was a kaleidoscope of coloured lights, spinning faster and faster as the sound rose to a deafening volume. Kneeling upright on the bed I was supported in perfect balance directly in the centre of the display. I felt completely calm and at peace and everything was refreshed and new. The questions flooded my mind again: 'Am I awake? Should I move?

How is this possible? Is this really happening?' Yet I knew that it was.

I could feel the discomfort of kneeling, my knees pressed into the mattress. I was inside a glowing canopy of unimaginable beauty, with a power surging around me and then through me. I wanted to move but I dared not. What would happen if I did? I was afraid it might disappear. As I listened, the whooshing sound changed, almost as if it slowed but then the tempo would increase again. Wow! My awareness had heightened. My bedroom had opened up even more and the colours were brighter. My skin felt cool and tingly. The sensations I felt were quite indescribable. I couldn't believe this was happening. It was lovely and I could have stayed there forever.

As I watched, the display began to take on a different appearance as the colour began to fade, back to that original pale, like when it first started.

Then the circle developed into a big cone shape and I was in the centre of it. Silent and peaceful but I could hear the sound of the whooshing around me very faintly. This place definitely had a presence all of its own. And then suddenly it was gone.

I could still faintly hear that whooshing sound as the thrilling display slowly and gently retreated back into the ceiling until all that was left was a very small coloured dot on my ceiling.

Slowly I sat back onto my feet. I was very relaxed and the room felt calm but I looked around in disbelief, wondering what had just taken place. I tried to orientate myself but had lost all sense of time. I had no idea how long I'd been there, on my knees, looking up into that magical space above my bed. Sitting there in the dark, exhausted and confused, I lay down, reached for a blanket and was asleep before my head touched the pillow.

The next morning I woke refreshed, as if I had enjoyed an uninterrupted sleep. I lay there for some time, staring at the ceiling, trying to make sense of the night before and feeling quite humble. As I went about my morning I was preoccupied with trying to work out how and why and who I could tell. There was no way I could tell the salon girls, they'd think I had lost my mind! I just couldn't keep this to myself. How would I ever explain what had happened to someone else? I imagined people's reactions were I to try to describe it and soon realised that I didn't have many choices - it had to be someone who knew me well and whom I could trust.

All day I racked my brains, trying to think who I could tell. I knew it would be an unusual conversation to say the least. As I worked, it suddenly came to me; I would talk to Colin and Elaine. Why hadn't I thought of them before?

I had known Colin and Elaine for years and together we had spent many a night sat around a table, putting the world to rights. They knew me well and would know that I would never tell them anything like this unless it really had taken place. But what would I say - and how and when? It needed to be as soon as possible, so I asked if I could visit them that night. I figured that with such short notice, they would know that something was wrong and would hopefully be free. I called Colin and explained that it was important I spoke with him urgently. Without hesitation he invited me over after work, I was so relieved!

The rest of the working day went smoothly but I found it difficult to concentrate. My mind was elsewhere, as I tried to figure out what I had seen and felt, and how I would describe it to someone else. When I finally closed the salon doors that day, I was overwhelmed with an unfamiliar anxiety. I drove straight to Colin and Elaine's house, using the twenty minute journey to gather my thoughts on how I would approach them with all of this. As I parked the car, I took deep breaths and decided that I should start explaining from the beginning, slowly working through to the end of the path, step by step. That way, they would know that I was telling the truth and that I hadn't gone crazy.

Satisfied that I had pulled myself together and was calm enough to sound reasonable, I rang the doorbell. Elaine answered and as soon as I stepped over the threshold, it all came flooding out; I didn't even stop to take a breath! Colin told me to slow down and start from the beginning again. This time, I explained in great detail, from the moment I had fallen asleep last night until I had woken this morning. There was silence as I tried desperately to read their faces; I needed some sort of validation that my mind was still intact. To my relief, they were fascinated and insisted on hearing every little detail all over again. Then came the questions, and after that we bounced around different theories as to why and how. I told them that I had chosen to talk to them because I knew they wouldn't laugh at me or think I was crazy. How grateful I was for that. Of all the theories we came up with that evening, the one that rang most true to me was Colin's conclusion that it was some sort of preparation. I would later find out just how right he was.

A few months previously, my 18 year-old daughter Lucy had gone on holiday with a friend. When she returned home she had a small amount of water blisters on her toes but I didn't worry unduly as I assumed they would disappear on their own. But as the weeks went on, she complained of them becoming very itchy and many more blisters appeared. Her feet started to swell and soon the blisters had spread all over the bottoms of her feet. Repeated visits to the doctor and many different creams did little to help and eventually the blisters became so bad that I felt she needed to see a skin specialist to find the source of the infection. Despite a series of visits to the dermatologist and various tests, the cause remained unknown. We even took in several pairs of her shoes to see if the glue or the lining could be to blame but nothing gave us the answers we sought and the infection continued to ravage her feet.

By then, Lucy could hardly walk and we feared that she would lose all the skin from the soles of her feet. She had suffered with these spreading blisters for almost 3 months and still we were no closer to finding either the cause or a cure. It seemed that the only option left was to apply steroid cream and hope for the best. At around 10pm on Thursday 21st September, I was preparing to settle down to bed when Lucy came into my bedroom whimpering like a little puppy. Her feet were very swollen and sore. Sitting upright against the headboard, I asked Lucy to sit with me; she was exhausted, in pain and in need of comfort. She hardly ever left the house and whenever she stood, her feet would crack and the skin would bleed.

That night, as we sat together on my bed, I asked Lucy to remove all the bandages and sit opposite me so that I could examine her feet closely. I had no idea how to help her but, like any mum, I instinctively wanted to do something. For reasons unknown to me, I felt compelled to put my hands over Lucy's feet, hovering just above without touching them. As I did so, Lucy exclaimed, "Mum, you're burning my feet!" I took my hands away and she said, "Look at your hands". I looked down and was taken aback to find that my hands were purple, as if I had gloves on. Lucy described a feeling of freezing cold air moving in between her toes and as she said that I felt an icy chill creeping up my left arm, around the back of my shoulders and down my right arm. It was like a freezing cold circle all around me. Slowly, we began to explore this invisible icy force.

The further I moved my hands outside the circle, the colder it became, so I kept my hands inside the middle of it. I didn't know what was happening but I knew it wasn't normal, or at least it didn't fall within the realms of what I considered normal. I thought back to the other night but could not remember either any freezing cold air around me or feeling very hot. But somehow I knew that it was all connected and I could tell by that feeling in the room that I had felt it before. This time it was much closer, almost standing next to me; no one was there but it just felt so right.

The look of astonishment that Lucy gave me confirmed everything to me. I still hadn't told her anything about the other night as I didn't want to scare her. After a few minutes, I realised it was happening again and Lucy's feet started to visibly change from red hot and swollen to very cold and almost white. The bedroom began to change even more and I am sure we both felt the presence, although neither of us mentioned it as I don't think we knew what to say.

That night we had a guest staying with us. He must have heard our excitement because he tried to come into the room, and was physically ejected by his solar plexus. Shocked, he did not try again but asked what was happening. We told him that we didn't know but he obviously considered himself excluded and retreated to bed; there was no way that the presence was going to allow him into the bedroom! The room took on the same sort of pale colour and I recognised it floating around the room, but this time it was not on the ceiling and did not last so long. It must have been 4am by the time Lucy and I finally fell asleep. The cleansing had begun, although I wasn't sure what had occurred between my daughter and me that night.

Although I'd had only a few hours sleep, when I woke for work the next morning I felt well rested. But I was quiet, which for me is unusual in itself. At the salon, it seemed a normal, lively Friday. I had a very good team of girls and we all worked well together, but something started to happen. It was September and the heating was on, as were the dryers that we used on our clients' hair, so a lot of heat was generated when all of us worked at the same time. But that day, there was something different, something unusual. I kept seeing silver lines, almost circling me. It was most odd, like very fine silvery-blue lines every time I worked next to or walked past a radiator.

All day I kept seeing them and by the afternoon, I decided to turn down the heating to see if that would make a difference. I wondered if it was because of the radiators or the hairdryers or whether there really was a show of colour that seemed to be following me. By the end of the day I just wanted to get home. Friday was our late night and after the shop had been cleaned and made ready to start afresh the next day, I would usually get home between six and seven.

Arriving home, I headed straight for the kitchen to prepare the evening meal. Tired, hungry and determined to have an early night, I started to cook. As I walked towards the cooker, there they were, the silvery-blue lines, swirling right in front of me.

I had been too busy in the salon that afternoon to have a good look at them but now that I was home, I wanted to understand what was happening. I tried to touch them but they quickly vanished. I was bewildered but I didn't feel uneasy; in fact, I felt unexpectedly calm. That night, I ate my food and went straight to bed; I had definitely had enough for one day.

The following day, it was a relief when nothing unusual happened. No icy sensations up my arms and no silvery-blue swirling lines. It was a typical Saturday at the salon, with a full appointment book up until 5pm. After closing, we all helped to clean up so that we could get home for the weekend. With everything else ready for Monday, I was about to cash up when I began to see those silvery-blue lines again, just like the day before. I paused and tried to work out what it was that I was seeing. All sorts of thoughts flashed through my mind: 'I'm not going to look. It's just my eyes playing tricks on me'.

It seemed that every time I was near a heat source, the lines would reappear, although I hadn't seen them all day. While I still hadn't figured out what they were, I knew they must be connected to that first night and to what had occurred while I was looking at Lucy's feet. I tried to put it to the back of my mind so I could finish closing the salon. I was at the cash register when the door opened and a woman I did not know walked in. Standing by the door, she looked straight at me and said "I've come to see you. I'm dying and I need your help". I looked at her in disbelief and said, "Why do you think I can help you?"

The woman didn't say another word and the salon went quiet. The girls who were still there had stopped what they were doing and just stared at me. Finally, one of them said, "Anne, why is she here asking you for help? What can you do? What does she mean?" I had no idea but I knew I needed to talk to this woman. I told the girls that they should leave and that I would see them on Monday. They were very hesitant, not wanting to leave me alone with this stranger after such an alarming request. But somehow I knew I needed to speak with the woman privately and so, reassuring the girls that I would be fine, I finally convinced them to go home with the promise that I would talk with them on Monday. Once they had left, I locked the door.

Alone with the stranger, I asked her why she had come to me. She said she didn't know why, she just knew it was me that she was supposed to go to. She knew I could help her. Suddenly I understood what I was supposed to do. I didn't comprehend how or why but I didn't hesitate either. I invited her upstairs to the room we used as a beauty room. There was a couch up there that I could use for her to lie down on. As we sat down to talk, the woman told me that she had a very bad pancreas problem and that the doctors had told her she was going to die. There was nothing they could do for her. She said she needed my help. I didn't understand how someone could just walk in to a shop and approach a perfect stranger but fortunately for us both, that is exactly what had happened.

Recalling the event with Lucy on Thursday night, I asked the woman to lie down on the couch. As she did, I began to move my hands until they hovered just centimetres above her abdomen. I knew by the feeling I was getting that there was a density under my hands, a sort of glue-like substance. It felt just like I was holding a sponge; it was quite bizarre. It was this that was stopping one of her organs from working correctly and I knew that I had to get it out so I just followed my instincts. It felt as though

I had placed my hand into a jar of treacle and then tried to remove it. Although there was nothing to be seen, I could feel the resistance as I tried to pull it away.

As I worked silently at the air above her abdomen, the lady commented, "I can feel something moving inside me". Suddenly an intense heat began to be released from the area as her muscles started to relax and move again, almost with a sense of relief at being set free. Somehow I knew I had to keep my hands in the right position to keep the energy going through, as I felt I wasn't yet reaching the heart of it. It felt like I was fighting the negative energy that was being produced in the abdomen and covering one of her organs, stopping it from functioning correctly. It was this negative energy that felt like glue under my hands and I knew that I needed to remove or dissolve it as soon as possible. I had to carry on until I was satisfied that I had removed it all.

I worked on the stranger for hours and then, as quickly as it had started, I knew my work was complete as I felt the change. It felt as though it was clear all the way through and I knew I had finished. The woman knew too and she sat up almost immediately. We sat and talked for ages about everything that had taken place. It had taken over three hours and we both knew it was finished; that was bizarre. Driving home, I reflected on what had just happened; I couldn't believe all the events of the last few days. I felt totally confused. It all seemed very surreal and even though I couldn't make sense of what was happening to me, by the time I got home I felt more relaxed and peaceful inside.

Lucy was at home waiting for me. I had barely walked in the door before she came bounding across the room towards me. "Look at my feet, Mum!" she cried excitedly. I looked down at her naked feet. She was no longer wearing the bandages that had hindered her for more than three months. I sat down to examine her. There was not a single blister on either of her feet. I couldn't believe it. The only indication that there had ever been anything wrong with her feet was just a little tiny mark where the skin had broken. I didn't know how to respond. I was delighted to have my happy girl back after she had been through so much. I was overwhelmed.

Lucy asked, "Where have you been?" and I didn't know how to begin. Taking a deep breath, I said, "We were really busy in the salon, as usual for a Saturday and I was just about to cash up when this woman came in". I told her what the woman had said. "Do you think it has something to do with what happened on Thursday night, Mum?". "Well, I believe so. It's just too much of a coincidence". It was then that I went on to tell Lucy about the thin silvery-blue lines I'd been seeing. We sat in silence, trying to make sense of the last several days. Neither of us knew what to make of it.

The next day was Sunday. In our home, Sundays were spent catching up from the week before and preparing for the week ahead. As I cleaned the house, did the washing and cooked for the week ahead, I could not help but wonder whether any more strange events would occur. Nothing did and in that sense it was a very quiet day, although that was to change by Tuesday afternoon.

Monday morning came and Lucy and I arrived at the salon at my usual time, about 7.45am. I drank my coffee as I prepared for the day ahead. The girls came in at 9am and straight away, they wanted to know about the woman who had come in at closing time on Saturday.

At first all I could tell them was that there was something going on that I didn't understand. They pressed me further so I began by telling them about Lucy and the events surrounding that Thursday night. They had seen how bad her feet were as she'd often come to the salon with me. Then I asked Lucy to take off her shoes. She showed the girls how her feet had healed. I don't think they would have believed it had they not seen it with their own eyes. That's when the questions started. I went on to tell them about the silvery-blue lines that had been swirling around me and then finally the details of the woman from Saturday night.

They seemed more accepting of Lucy's story. That, in part, was due to the fact that she was standing right there and they could see her recovery for themselves. The rest of my accounts were met with some scepticism. I understood their hesitation to take it all in; these unexplainable events were so bizarre I could hardly believe them myself. I kept thinking to myself, 'Girl, you have lost it'. It was all too much to grasp and to try to make sense of. But Monday passed and I arrived home without any further events. It was a great feeling and I hoped that maybe things were starting to get back to normal.

Tuesday morning started slowly. My first client wasn't due for a while, so it gave me a chance to enjoy my coffee and catch up with myself. I was still upstairs when my client arrived. After one of the girls had shampooed her hair, I came down. We hadn't seen this lady before, but all were welcome. She was having a shampoo and set and I noticed that she had brought a pillow with her. Settling her in a chair, ready for me to set her hair, I commented on the pillow. She told me that she had an ongoing back problem and was seeing her chiropractor again that afternoon.

As I started to put in the rollers, my eyes looked straight at the back of the lady's head and straight down her spine. To this day, I don't know why I did that but that was all I did. When she was sat under the dryer, I went back upstairs to finish my coffee. It did not once occur to me that I might have done anything by focusing my eyes on the back of her neck. Once her hair had been set and the rollers removed, I styled the lady's hair and she left. About an hour later, the phone rang. It was her. Straight away she asked, "What did you do to me?"

She told me that on the way to her car, a voice inside her head asked why she was walking the way she did. Since leaving the salon, she had felt no pain whatsoever and felt better than she had in months. When she went home, she told her husband about it and, as if to demonstrate, she did the twist in the kitchen, right in front of him. The lady's husband thought she had gone completely mad! "All this happened after I'd been to your salon," she said. "I'm going to see my chiropractor this afternoon. He will know if something has happened to my back and be able to explain". She promised to ring me when she had seen the chiropractor. I was speechless; utterly amazed by what I had heard. What did I do? What on earth was happening with me? I didn't have a clue.

I waited all afternoon for her to phone and in the end I didn't think she was going to. But just as we were about to close the salon and go home, the lady called. She had seen her chiropractor. He had examined her thoroughly, confirmed that her back had repaired itself and said that he didn't need to see her again. I simply couldn't believe it; I was bewildered. When the same lady came in again a week later to have her hair done, she told everybody in the salon what had taken place.

This was just the start of what was to come; what was happening to me was quite unbelievable. So much had happened in such a short time and I was quite overwhelmed by it all. As word spread of my healing work and success rate, people began approaching me with all sorts of ailments and I was happy to do whatever I could to help them. I didn't yet know what I was capable of doing. Everyone wanted to know how I was achieving these amazing things but I knew that I could not mention that first night, so I decided to say nothing at all. But I did my best to help whoever asked for my help. That was, and still is, all that I can do.

The speed with which my healing progressed left me struggling to take it all in. The next incredible event took place in the salon on the Thursday afternoon, just two days after I had met the lady with the back problem. We had all worked very hard that day, without breaking for lunch. It was 4pm and there was only one client left in the salon, so I sent the girls upstairs to rest up.

The lady sat at the wash basin waiting for me. In my early days as a hairdresser, I used to love shampooing; making sure that my client was all tucked in so that I didn't get her wet. Once the water reached the right temperature, I began wetting the lady's hair, ready to apply the shampoo. As I started to work the shampoo in with my fingers, she remarked on a funny reaction, saying, "Well, I've never felt that before". Oh no, I thought, not now. I asked what she meant. "Well, it's like pins and needles coming down the side of my face and going in to my neck and shoulder. Now it's in my arm". That was when I asked whether she had a problem with her arm. When she replied that she did, you can imagine what I was thinking. The sensation began working its way through the lady's right arm and she said that she had never felt anything like it.

It turned out she had been a nurse at a local hospital but had had to leave due to an injury sustained from lifting a patient. Her right arm had been badly injured and she'd had only limited use of the limb for years. As I washed her hair, she described a feeling of something being moved inside. The sensations she experienced felt very strange and extended from her head right down the neck, into the shoulder and then into the arm. While I dried her hair, she described feeling that the arm was being worked on and said that she could feel everything that was happening. Once her hair was finished and her next appointment made, the lady agreed to ring me if she felt worried and left the salon.

In the meantime, word of my healing continued to spread and many more people asked me about it. It was quite overwhelming at times, especially as everything seemed to be happening so fast. I began to wonder whether I could cope with it all, but being a pragmatic sort of person, I decided that I had to be able to cope otherwise it wouldn't have happened to me. The following week arrived and the lady was due. Thankfully, the salon was busy and I didn't have too much time to dwell on things. When the door opened and she walked in, I had no idea what to expect. We smiled at one another and she asked if she could have a word with me. My heart was in my mouth, but I need not have worried because her beaming smile said it all.

"You'll never guess what I've been doing" she said. "All weekend, I've cleaned out my kitchen cupboards from top to bottom and my arm has been fabulous. I've got no pain whatsoever and I haven't taken a single painkiller since I saw you last week. I just can't believe it!" I was equally amazed and told her how happy I was for her. She told me that her husband could not believe the difference in her. She had been dependent on painkillers since the accident but no longer needed them, not even to go to sleep. "Thank you" she said, "Thank you so much. I don't know what you did but you did something and I cannot thank you enough".

Later that same day, the woman from that first Saturday came back, accompanied by her family who wanted to meet me. It seemed that the healing had worked and that the problem with her pancreas was no longer life threatening. She said that she had felt extremely well and had no pain. Her doctor was amazed. She now says that she has never looked back after her healing with me that Saturday night when she walked into the salon. She still does not know why she felt that she had to come but is so glad that she did. I still ask myself how she knew; I suppose it's just one of the wonders of the events that have taken place.

We became friends and I was invited to her home for dinner. Sometimes we would go out for food. I did her hair regularly and members of her family would come to the salon. I got to know her well and I met her dear mum. But something inside my head seemed to be warning me about becoming too close. For a while I had a funny sort of feeling that it wasn't to be and that I had to learn to be self sufficient. I knew I was being pulled back, not only from her but from many of my long standing friends as well. But they all understood how I felt about my work. They knew that because I was working all sorts of hours and long days, I needed to catch my breath but that I would always be there if they needed me.

I felt that I was being shown a new path, one that I had no choice but to just follow and listen to the teachings that came my way. These, it seemed, didn't include this lovely lady; she was now healed and there were many more for me to see, so I had to pull away from her. I felt very sad for her but it was the right way; she had received her healing and has never looked back. I saw her a while ago with her grandchildren. It was lovely to see her and one day I will explain to her why I had to pull back but in the meantime I wish her well.

By this time, there was so much happening around me, so much that I needed to concentrate on. I kept seeing different pictures in my mind. I didn't realise at that time that I was already ahead of myself and so my next task was completely unexpected. It seemed that I was to have company on my journey, all of which had to be created by me. I felt compelled to draw and the pictures that I would create would be my company. All these different drawings were ready and waiting for me to create and I knew that it was going to be hard work even to find the right paper for the series of drawings that were continually being shown to me.

The pictures in my mind were really strong and clear. I knew they had to be exactly right and that there was no margin for error, even down to the exact shade of charcoal to give the impact that was required. It took a while before I was satisfied with my choice but eventually I found the materials I needed in an art shop in the city and I was ready. When I arrived home that night it was too late to start, so I had dinner and went to bed. As I settled down for a good night's sleep, I realised I was being taken up into the universe, as I have been countless times, but this time I was taken up into the stars and vast space.

Closing my eyes it felt like I was travelling like a speeding light. One minute everything was all black and then suddenly a huge crack appeared in the pure black and an array of amazing colours came flooding through, just like when the sun comes through the clouds but the ray of light that burst through was pure colour. Every colour you could think of in one massive explosion. It felt like I was experiencing colour like never before, right across my vision and I could hardly keep my eyes open. It was the most amazing sight I have ever seen. I felt like screaming; it was so amazing. I knew there and then that this would be my first drawing, although I didn't yet know how I was going to draw it. How was I ever going to recreate the most amazing thing I had ever seen?

At that time, I was living with Janet, my sister. I didn't see her the next morning as she was always in work by 6am. I got up and got ready for work as normal, thinking of what I was going to do when I got home and wondering if I could do the drawing. I made sure I wasn't late getting home from work because I needed to chat to Jan, to let her know what I was doing. When I told her that I needed to draw in the bedroom, she asked why. I explained that I didn't yet know but that I had a theory. She gave her blessing and offered me an old sheet to put over the bed to stop the charcoal from making a mess. I was ready to start.

My bedroom looked out over the school and the rolling fields beyond. You could see for miles, so I had the perfect outlook. Before starting the drawing I sorted my room out, but there was one problem: I knew the sheet wasn't going to cover a lot. However, I was very eager to start, so to keep it from slipping, I put the paper on to a board that Jan's husband had given me and set to work on my very first drawing. I got totally carried away and at one point I started to laugh - my hands were working madly and I forgot myself for a while, but I soon came around when I saw the mess I had made. That first night, I just couldn't believe the mess I had to clean up. It took me longer to clean up than to do the drawing!

CHAPTER TWO – The Energy Circle

My life as I knew it was seriously changing, and at such a rapid pace. There were new surprises nearly every day. Something would happen and I never knew what the day would bring. It was very different from how, as a young girl growing up in Penarth, I had imagined my life would be. Nevertheless, my salon was well known and successful, so that gave me a degree of continuity. I have always lived in Penarth. I went to school here and dreamed of becoming a hairdresser from an early age. I started a part time job at a local salon at the age of thirteen and when I left school, I was offered a permanent post, so I was on my way to achieving my dream.

I am dyslexic, however, there was no name for this when I was young. I knew that I would have to work twice as hard to ensure that my dyslexia did not hold me back. I thought that if I could hide it then no one would find out. The owner of the salon insisted on making all the appointments herself, I was there to clean and wash towels day after day. I even had blisters on my hands, but I didn't care. I didn't mind how much I worked as long as I became a hairdresser. When I started to shampoo, I dreamed of having my very own salon but before that happened I had to work hard and gain a lot of experience.

I finally opened my salon in the eighties. I left the salon I had been working in for thirteen years and took the plunge, starting on my own with my daughter Lucy helping after school and on weekends. Soon I needed more staff so I phoned a girl who I used to work with and offered her a job. And so my little salon was born and I never looked back. Weekends were our busiest times but most of our clients preferred to make appointments, so we usually had a good idea of what to expect. Some would phone that day and others would take a chance and just come in. Others came in just to look at the new hairstyle books but we welcomed everyone and most of our clients enjoyed a cup of tea or coffee and a good chat, which was the sort of happy and relaxed atmosphere I wanted.

We always made people feel welcome and very rarely had any problems. If a client treated one of the girls disrespectfully, then I would ask them to leave but thankfully that sort of thing didn't happen often. The girls that worked with me were the best. Some had moved with me from previous salons, so we had a long-standing relationship. I worked with one stylist for over eighteen years. Another, who originally started with me as a Saturday girl, actually took over the salon when I decided to do my healing from home. That was a major decision for me. I was very lucky to have had a good team of not only staff but clients as well. Many people used my little salon and I loved it. I never thought anything could tear me away from it - but then I never imagined this sort of change could ever happen to me or anyone else.

I was experiencing so many different things on a daily basis. There seemed to be no let up. I had to pinch myself so that I knew it was me and that I wasn't dreaming. I still saw the fine lines that had appeared the week before, but not as often because I tried to stay away from the radiators! The events of the previous week were still very fresh in my mind. It seemed that I was waiting for the door to open and the next surprise to enter. I wanted to see more and I knew there was more to come. In such a short space of time, I felt that it had become a part of me. There was an urge to know more, to be shown how it all worked. Somehow, I knew that I did not have to concern myself as to how I was going to be taught. I felt at peace with myself.

I was living with my sister Janet while I found somewhere that I could live and work. I had found the perfect place but it had been totally abused by the previous occupant. It wasn't nice at all but I could see the potential. I had to get it ready and I knew that it was going to take some time to make it homely and suitable. I had the feeling that a lot had happened there and I could sense something, so I wanted to make sure I did as much as possible to get rid of whatever it was I could feel there before I moved in. And of course there was so much still happening around me at that time. The colours were just so demanding; they were changing all the time and I was starting to see all sorts of shapes.

My emotions were all over the place. I was still in the salon, trying to get used to staying with my sister, working frantically to get my new home ready and sleeping in the universe every night, so it was no wonder I was seeing things. The colours were whooshing and the shapes were changing into pictures. I was not sure where they were coming from, but they were changing into real pictures. It was simply amazing; if I had told a doctor all that was going on, I am sure that I would have been committed. Perhaps I should have gone; at least I would have had a chance to rest!

My poor sister didn't know what to make of it all, and so she asked one of her friends to come and have a chat with me. To be honest, I was glad for someone to chat with. Her name was Doreen and my sister had told her everything, so she was coming over that night. She apparently knew all about the sort of things that were happening to me and I couldn't wait to leave work. When I got home, Doreen was in the kitchen chatting with my sister. As soon as she saw me, she asked, "What are they doing to you, Anne?" I replied that I had no idea but that I needed to know what was happening to me as I had never experienced anything like it.

That evening, Doreen told me about the Spiritualist church. For a long time, she had attended regularly and had heard many visiting mediums. She told me about the healers who give up their time to see the people who come for help with their different ailments. Sometimes there would be more healers than people who needed healing and so the healers would work together on the same person.

I had never heard about it. I didn't know anything like that even existed. Doreen suggested that perhaps I needed to see for myself but I politely declined, saying that it wasn't for me. I still wasn't sure what was happening but I didn't think that was what I needed at all, although I respected that some people needed the comfort that they derived from the church. I thanked Doreen for the invitation and asked if we might talk again. She readily agreed and offered to bring some leaflets from the Spiritualist church so that I could read for myself.

Before leaving, she told me, "When spirits work with you, Anne, it's a wow. They channel through you. You become a vessel for the energy to travel through you". I said that reminded me of my mother, who had told me that I was empty; that I had nothing there. "That's what they call it: channelling the energy that comes from the universe down through you and into the person you're giving healing to. The person receiving the healing gets better, as easy as that. At least, it sounds easy but not everyone who says they can do it is any good. Often the healers who doubt their ability are the best". I thanked Doreen and arranged to see her again.

It was such a relief to have spoken to someone who had some idea of what was going on in my mind. At least I knew I wasn't going nuts. She knew about the colours. That was the moment that I became calm. And then hearing about spirits: I thought I would understand one day, but it suited me at the moment to stay ignorant. I wasn't going to give myself any pressure at all. I know my family and friends were not sure at all because of the big change in me and I was trying not to tell them everything. If they really knew what was happening they would have been even more anxious and I didn't want that to happen.

I was really looking forward to talking with Doreen again. She helped me to know that I wasn't alone and she understood what I was going through. We had such a good chat when she came over. I told her that things were just going too fast and how I felt compelled to draw. She brought a lot of information that told me about the church that she went to, about what happened there and how it all worked. It was not for me but it was very interesting. Doreen and I had many chats and lots of laughs and she really helped me in the early days when I did not know anything. God bless her.

I felt I had so much more insight into personal things that had previously happened. I explained to Lucy that she wasn't to worry and that everything was going to be okay. We had put up with a lot over the past nine months, before all this started, but that was all behind us now. I am sure that it had a lot to do with why this happened to me and perhaps when the time is right, I will write about it.

I was so pleased that Lucy was over all that nasty stuff with her feet. I didn't see much of her at the time as she had a lot of catching up to do in her life. The difference in her was amazing and she had no more problems at all; she was back to having a good time with friends and I could concentrate on the next stage of my work.

I wanted to look more closely at all the colours and the drawings that I was seeing. They were very pale but when I concentrated, I felt a new level of awareness. I knew there was a lot more to this and I was going to try and find out. I had to draw although I didn't know if I could. I was seeing the changes in the colours. I would have to wait and see what was going to happen that night when I closed my eyes; whether I would be whisked away into the universe like I had been for the last few weeks. It was impossible to try and quantify the power behind that work. The things I was seeing just defied belief. I was seeing all these beautiful colours and such fantastic shapes, the colours mixed together were just amazing. Yes, it sounds mad, I know. But it was like I was being catapulted into a dimension that was not altogether of this world.

Some of the people that I was seeing had not used my salon before, but had heard of my healing work through others. One of the girls in the salon put me in touch with a man who had been a healer for many years. He had known about different sorts of healing since childhood. I was so pleased and I couldn't wait to go and see him. He was a teacher at a local school, so I felt I could trust him. He sounded really nice on the phone and reassured me that sometimes things happen the way they had with me. I arranged to meet him and I couldn't wait. I would have gone there and then if I hadn't been working in the salon that day.

When we finally met, it was such a relief to talk to someone who understood what I was experiencing and how fast it all seemed to be happening. I told him of the advice that I had been given - that I was to set examples and be taught how to heal. He replied that I would have my own teachers and no one else, explaining that the decision to give me this gift had come from the universe. He added that they would teach me everything that I needed to know and more and assured me that I would be well looked after.

Then he asked me a question. "If you were having a meal and someone phoned and asked for your help right away, would you finish your meal or would you have it later?" I thought for a minute and just looked at him. I said, "No, I'm sorry, I wouldn't put my meal down. I would have to finish it first and then I would go and help". He replied, "Very good answer. I asked you that question because you must remember to take good care of yourself first and rest when you have to".

I asked him about the colours that I was seeing and how long I would continue seeing them. "For your lifetime," he replied. I asked how he had known about his gift. "It was part of my childhood. It was always there with me". I remarked that he seemed very relaxed. "Yes, it's been part of me all this time, because we are born to it. It is part of you now, that's why you are here, to show people the way, like myself. You must have had a great injustice done to you to have this so late in your life. It's going to be hard work," he replied. I said that I had worked hard all my life and that I wasn't worried about that.

He explained how he had handled all the incoming information. "The way they teach us comes in thought. You know when you remember something? How do you think that happens?" I thought about his question for a moment. "Well I think it just comes, everyone does it, don't they?" I said. "Yes they do," he replied, "but we have help. Know when you're reminded of something that it's your guide that is helping you". I asked what he meant. "We all have a guide," he told me. "They are there to help us, to guide us through our lives". I smiled at him. "I think I've worked that one out for myself with all that's happened to me over the last few months".

"The energy you are working with at the moment has nothing to do with your guides; that is a different thing all together. You have a gift given to you and you will have your own teachers, but you must learn to shut yourself down at night otherwise you won't get much rest. They will want to talk to you all the time. Our guides come with us when we are born and leave when we die. They are there to help us". I asked him how this could be when people were unaware of it. He replied, "Because it's for each of us to find out and people are learning all the time".

I asked him about the people that don't believe in this sort of thing. He said, "That's the choice we make for ourselves. We don't all have to be the same; we're here to learn for ourselves. Does it feel like someone is talking to you in your mind?" I just looked at him then said, "Oh well that's it then, I've gone nuts". "No Anne, it's not like that. But you will be guided through all the things you have to learn". "Thank you," I said. "All you have told me today has given me so much help". "This is only the start; you have a long way to go yet, and a lot to learn. But never join any organisation; you have to stay on your own. When they find out what you can do, they will all want you". "Okay," I promised. "You will be all right, you don't need any one else to help you Anne. They will show you everything you need to know, don't worry".

I asked him if he knew how long it would take for me to understand all that I needed to know. He replied, "You will always be learning Anne, it won't stop. But you will have to learn to switch off otherwise you will leave yourself open to energies that are around us. It will take time for you to learn". I left the teacher's home feeling much better equipped to deal with what was happening to me. I understood a bit more of what was going on. I knew that if it carried on at this rate, I would have to sort out a different way of working.

Ironically, I received a visitor at the salon the very next day, wanting me to join the World Federation of Healers. I just smiled and of course I refused, but to this day I still have the form that he left with me 'just in case I changed my mind'. That was nearly fifteen years ago and I often think of that long chat with the teacher and the advice that I so desperately needed. I would like to say a big thank you to a very clever man for all the time and help that he gave me. I continued with my healing and was very careful to follow his advice.

With the help of not only the girls, but the clients as well, we found a new way for me to work in the salon, with everyone helping me to achieve what I needed. I worked as a hairdresser in the morning and finished at 2pm. After that, I would go upstairs to receive the people who needed healing. There was a constant demand and I did not charge for my work. I would stay upstairs for as long as necessary. At times, I didn't finish until very late but if the people came to see me and I had a space then I would see them. People came from all over and the healing that took place was extraordinary.

I was being taught and guided just like the teacher had said I would be. Who would have thought I could do this and that someone or something was definitely helping me. I must have been doing it right otherwise I wouldn't have had so many people coming to me. And it did not seem to matter what ailments I was presented with because I felt that I would be shown what was needed. The new working pattern that the girls and I had devised seemed to suit us all and I felt greatly supported. I still wasn't sure how the girls felt about my healing though, so I included them whenever possible to help them adjust to the changes that were taking place around them.

As for the clients, one lady in particular caught my eye. Her name was May and I felt that she wanted to speak with me. I had noticed that she had been coming in a bit earlier than her appointment so she could chat with other clients. I thought she needed the company and knew she had made friends with some of the clients that came at the same time as her. My salon was a place for people to meet and fulfil their social needs and I enjoyed listening to them chatting about the past week and their plans for the days ahead.

One Friday morning in late January, May arrived just in time for her appointment. That was very unusual as she always came early for her morning chat with her friends. As she walked in, she greeted everyone as normal and went to speak to the stylist who usually did her hair.

The stylist called me over and asked if I would have a word with May about her husband, Fred. The poor man had had a stroke a few years before and was having a bad time of it. May told me that just lately Fred wasn't the same. He was usually quite upbeat and social, even after his stroke, but in recent months he seemed to be really down. He didn't want to leave the house much anymore and he was losing interest in everything. His ability to accomplish daily tasks was declining rapidly and May no longer felt comfortable leaving him alone. He was slowly declining physically and emotionally. Because he could not pick up his leg, Fred dragged it behind him when he walked and was wearing out one of his shoes. I was sad to hear that he was in such a state. May had come to ask for my help and I was determined to do my utmost to help her and Fred. We made an appointment for him for the following Thursday after the salon had closed.

Once May had left, I was concerned that Fred might not be able to get upstairs to the beauty room that had become my healing room. The only way up was via a metal spiral staircase and I didn't know how Fred would manage to climb it if the muscles in his arm and leg had wasted as May had described. I knew that we would have to find a way, as I didn't have another private area in which to treat him. Thursday came around quickly and I had arranged with the girls that they would all leave at 5pm, lock the door, and put the keys through the letterbox. When Fred arrived, I don't think he knew what to expect and to be honest, neither did I. All I knew was that I was going to make sure he was given the best healing session possible.

I explained to Fred that the healing room was upstairs and offered to help him but the dear chap insisted on pulling himself up the stairs all on his own. He was so determined and while it pained me to see him struggle, I couldn't insist that he let me help him. I suspected that his declining independence was partially to blame for how low he had been feeling lately. I just let him get on with it while I tidied up the salon and a short time later I followed him upstairs. Fred was sitting on the stool in the hallway when I got to the top. I was impressed with his determination. Smiling I said, "Well done darling, you made short work of those stairs. Come on in Fred, this used to be our beauty room but I've got it for my healing room now. A bit small, but it works. Tell me a bit about yourself Fred. How are you getting on?" After a few minutes of polite exchanges, Fred opened up and I was able to get a better impression of his concerns and his condition.

I think it is important for people to express themselves and to open up to me before we start any type of healing. While listening to my clients, I direct my questions to get to the root of their problem. The first couple of minutes will usually consist of my client just venting but, once that is done, we are able to move on to the deeper questions that will undoubtedly reveal the inner issue. It's through my understanding of the mind-body connection that I am able to source the emotional issue that is revealing itself physically. My technique does not suit all, but I seem to know when clients want to have a chat and when they need a bit more time to feel like they can open up to me. I wanted to hear from Fred primarily to explore how he felt about what had happened to him and how he had been dealing with it since. It was important for me to establish how mentally strong he was.

If I feel that a client does not have a particularly strong resolve, then I have a different approach. For instance, if the client is tired or rundown, then it's best to just put them straight into the colours so their mind can rest. But if I can coax them to talk a bit about what is going on in their lives first, then it helps to weaken the negative energy that has a hold on them, and it can be very revealing regarding the emotional side of their physical ailment. Fred had grown tired of his body not working properly, of losing his independence and of not being able to enjoy his life and the things that he loved. He felt so limited by his stroke that he was just giving up. From Fred's perspective, every day was a losing battle and he just didn't have it in him to fight anymore.

As he lay on the bed I started at his head, just to feel how much heat was there. From that point I can read the rest of the body by pushing energy down the spine and through to the feet. The only time it won't go straight through is if there is a blockage somewhere between the head and the feet. Fred reacted to my pushing the energy through him almost at once and I was not ready for how his body reacted to it. First his right arm lifted up and then went back down. Then his left arm followed, which surprised Fred since he wasn't able to lift his left arm on his own. The power of his arm coming up was almost like somebody was lifting it and then stretched it forward as far as it would go. Then they did exactly the same to the other arm. I had never seen anything like it, but I felt I should trust what the energy change in his body was carrying out. And then his right leg lifted and then his left, just as his arms had done.

Fred kept saying how nice it felt for his limbs to be lifted and stretched in that way, and then all of a sudden, Fred was lifted from the table! The only parts of him still touching the bed were the back of his head and neck and the soles of his feet, as if an imaginary cable was attached to the ceiling and wrapped around his midsection and he had been hoisted upward. I was in complete shock and I did not believe what I was seeing; I also didn't know what I was supposed to do about it. No sooner had those thoughts run through my mind when Fred exclaimed how wonderful it felt. Still in disbelief I replied, "It happens all the time". I couldn't believe I had just fibbed! I didn't know what to say as I had never seen anything like this and I didn't want to frighten him, so tried to act as if I'd seen this a million times.

Fred was then put back down on the bed just as unexpectedly and as gently as he'd been lifted. I continued with my hands still on him as I concentrated on moving the energy through his body again; although the remainder of the session was much less eventful. Two hours later I felt I had done all I could for that session so I quietly stood up and left the room. I walked out into the area which we called the staff room and I just leaned on one of the chairs in absolute shock. I heard Fred stirring so I hollered back into the beauty room, "I'll be there now Fred; I'm just going to wash my hands". Finishing at the sink, I wandered back into the beauty room. Fred was sat up and he looked quite lively. He said, "Anne that was brilliant! I want to come back next week!" I was beaming and so pleased Fred had found our session worth coming back for. "Yes, my darling, I'll make another appointment for you, I'll just go and make you a cup of tea now".

Fred and I sat and talked about all sorts of different things after a session, which of course are private, but I can tell you that once the shock had worn off, he was delighted. He said he felt so different, better in fact, both physically and mentally. I knew that purging him of both his negative feelings and his negative outlook made room for some positive energy to take its place. Because of the immediate results, I had won Fred's confidence, helping him to accept those strange events and to believe that what we had accomplished that day was not some form of magical witchcraft, but simply a manipulation of a person's energy. I was so happy Fred wanted to come back next week and that he felt better when he left and I was hungry to explore my newfound gift.

~~~0~~~

As Fred's next appointment drew near, I wondered what would happen if someone else witnessed his session. If it went as it did last time and I had a witness then I would have confirmation that I didn't imagine it all and that I wasn't going crazy. I still doubted myself because everything was happening so quickly and I needed time to take it all in. I thought about who I could trust. Instantly Mandy came to mind. She was one of my top stylists and we had worked together for years. I knew her to be trustworthy, discreet and honest. I approached her that Thursday, about an hour before Fred arrived. I was careful not to say specifically why I wanted her to watch his session, just that I needed her to be my witness. My vagueness must have made her curious because she agreed to stay.

When Fred arrived for his healing session he was in high spirits. He kept talking about how he had had such a good week. I was surprised that he didn't complain of being stiff or sore from the stretching and movements of last week's session, but he insisted that he felt better than he had in a long time and he had done more for himself and around the house that week as well. I was convinced that another session was just what Fred needed. "Off you go Fred; I'll be up shortly, just take a seat". I said giving him a few minutes to get upstairs before I went up. That's when I asked him if he would mind if one of my girls observed his healing session. "No my darling, as long as you do what you did last week it will be fine". And I thought Oh, yes, last week. Oh my God, what if it doesn't happen?

My mind was all over the place but I quickly calmed myself so that I could focus. I called down to Mandy and she came upstairs. By this time Fred was already laying down so I asked Mandy to sit on a stool just outside the door. I didn't think it was a good idea to have her directly in the room, but I was hoping exactly the same thing would happen so Mandy would experience the same event that had taken place the week before. I made sure to position her so she had a clear view because if it happened again, I didn't want her to miss a thing. I sat in my normal place at the head of the bed and put my hands on Fred's shoulders. In no time at all, Fred's right arm lifted, stretching out and up.

It was slightly different to the last time and I was worried that it wasn't going to happen again. But then his left arm did the same and shortly after his right leg and then his left leg, just like last time.

I sat perfectly still with my hands on his shoulders and really focused on pushing the energy through his body. Slowly but surely Fred lifted, just like the first time, except this time I could see he was much more relaxed. I'm sure it was because he felt that he was in safe hands. At this point I looked over to Mandy; her face had such a funny expression on it and her mouth was agape. She was white from shock. Although I already must have known what her answer would be, I mouthed to her, "Can you see this?" Mandy just nodded her head in agreement with that same look of shock still on her face. I also remember thinking how much strength it must take to hold him up in an arch like that. Fred remained in that position for several minutes and then just as gently as he was raised, he was lowered back down onto the bed. He was so relaxed and his eyes were closed so I stood up and walked out of the room, meeting Mandy at the doorway. We looked at each other but neither of us spoke as she was so shocked that she could not say a word. I suggested we talk in the morning.

I made the tea and Fred made another appointment for the following week. Fred knew he was in safe hands by this time, a place that he could trust even if it went beyond the realms of explanation! We agreed that even though we didn't fully understand it, we knew it was happening and we knew it was good. Fred said during the sessions he felt at peace and he felt cared for. Like when a small child is cradled in his mother's lap, encircled within loving arms; he is safe and all is right in the world. Fred described seeing colours: beautiful, vibrant and alive. I could see a sparkle in his eyes and could hear the enthusiasm in his voice. This man sitting next to me was an entirely different person to the man that had limped into my salon with a broken body, a broken heart and a defeated mind.

While I gave him healing, he could remember what it was like to be alive again. Fred told me how he was now able to feel anticipation welling up inside him, like when a day you have been looking forward to for ages finally arrives. And for the first time in years he felt hope. He was now able to see an abundance of possibilities in each day, the kind that negativity makes invisible. Fred was determined to continue feeling this way and he wanted to know if he could produce these feelings at home. I was so pleased with his willingness to contribute to his own healing. Before Fred left, I told him that participation in his own healing was crucial. He needed to fight to get his body back.

Fred would have to muster all the determination he could possibly manage and dig down deep. Not just believe that his mind, his thoughts, could create his future, but to know that they do. Now that Fred remembered what it felt like to really be alive, he would need to focus on those images and the feelings they evoked. The thoughts in your mind, I told him, develop into feelings and the result is energy. When you're at home and you're thinking about how much you're unable to do and all that has been taken from you, those thoughts progress into feelings; negative feelings of helplessness, despair and victimisation. Negative energy weakens and damages our physical body. But, if at home you focus on what you *can* do, what you *do* have, that positive energy mixed with gratitude is so important in recovery. Positive energy strengthens and replenishes our physical body. Grab hold of that positive energy and you will flourish.

I explained to Fred that he must stop living like he had a broken body, and behave as though he determined his own mobility. I knew his acceptance of this principle would greatly establish to what extent he would heal physically and emotionally. I also knew that this way of thinking was completely foreign to him. Having him come back for weekly healing would reinforce this new way of being. It would allow me to encourage him while he managed his own health and it would give him someone to share his progress with. Our sessions gave him a temporary reprieve from the struggles of recovering from a stroke, as well as enabling me to transfer to him a mega-dose of positive energy. When I pull the negative energy out of a client, it leaves a void in their energy field that I'm able to fill with positive energy. Positive energy begins healing on contact and as I unblock the energy flow in their body and push it through the current circulates, mending as it goes.

Mandy had seen everything, and that was exactly what I needed: affirmation from an uninvolved source. I had been swaying between disbelief and certainty since the moment I was given my gift. But self-doubt was now cast away; if I was delusional and hallucinating, Fred and Mandy wouldn't have experienced the events that they had. That affirmation was just what I needed to tip the balance in favour of my being able to accept this gift. My reality was now different than that of most others I knew. Realising this changed my mindset from doubt to determination to understand and develop my ability. I wondered who else was able to do what I do. I'd heard of 'faith healers' before. Maybe that's what this is? I made a note to myself to look into it, as I gathered my coat and purse. I remember how humble I felt as I drove home that night.

~~~0~~~

I always arrived at the salon at 7.45am so I could have a coffee before anyone came in. Sometimes there would be a client waiting outside for me and I would have to start early; other times no one would be waiting so I could have those few minutes to myself. As I neared the salon the anticipation of speaking with Mandy grew, even more so when I could see that the pavement was empty. I hurried upstairs and put the kettle on; she should be here any minute. While the kettle was boiling, I went over to the door of my healing room. I sat down on the stool where Mandy had sat. I could just imagine how it must have looked to her and the shock she must have felt to sit there and watch Fred being lifted like that. I heard the door open downstairs but it was another of the stylists. I didn't want to mention anything to her until after I had spoken to Mandy. She finally arrived just minutes before our first clients were due and as Fridays were always very busy, I realised I might have to wait to speak to her until after we had closed.

As I poured the three of us a cup of coffee, I could see from the corner of my eye that Mandy was watching me. She just would not stop looking at me and each time I met her gaze she would say, "I'm coming to see you over the weekend, we have to talk". I smiled. I welcomed the thought of being able to pore over all that had gone on. Since late September, my whole life had been turned upside down and no one really knew just how much. So many strange and wonderful things had taken place in just five months; I wondered what it would be like in a year or two. I had to force myself to stop trying to figure it all out, trying to plan and to ask why, how and what if? It was all too much to think about. I knew if I was going to embark on this path successfully, I would have to accept it, learn from it, and just let things happen.

That Friday, the salon was as busy as ever. I was disappointed about having to wait to speak with Mandy, but Fred's wife, May, always came in on Fridays. I brightened a little at the thought of hearing about Fred's progress. I needed to prepare myself in case May asked questions about my sessions with Fred. Confidentiality has always been paramount and I knew that my clients wouldn't open up and confide in me if they couldn't trust me, especially in a small town like Penarth. I decided that I wouldn't mention Fred's sessions and if she brought it up, I would be mindful of Fred's privacy.

When May arrived, she asked to speak to me. I was already with a client, so I suggested that she stay for a cup of tea once her hair was done. Later, we sat in the staff room with a cup of tea and I asked what was on her mind. After we had spoken for a few minutes, it was obvious that Fred had told her all about his experience during his healing session. She was delighted that there had been such a big improvement in his mental and physical state; however, she admitted she found it hard to believe what he'd told her about his arms and legs being pulled and stretched and about him being lifted from the bed. I confirmed that I had seen it with my own eyes and that Mandy had as well. I could tell from her expression that she didn't know what to believe.

I was all too familiar with that internal struggle between what we believe can and cannot happen. I told her that the only parts of Fred's body that had been touching the bed were the back of his head and neck, and the soles of his feet. She knew that he didn't have the strength to hold himself up in such a way, especially since his stroke. He was, after all, 73 years old and nearly paralysed on his left side. I was about to explain that he hadn't done it on his own, that he'd had help; that he hadn't lifted himself, he'd been lifted, but it occurred to me that maybe she wasn't ready to know just yet. Perhaps some things were just too much to comprehend. And did she really need to know how the healing was achieved? Her belief, or disbelief, in the method, had no effect on the outcome. So I simply said, "Well my dear, does it really matter how it works? All that matters is that he's improving and you two are happy with the results".

Such a simple, innocent statement, but the revelation of my own words hit me like a thunderbolt; I had to stop trying to answer the whys and hows of this gift. It would be so much easier if I just accepted that this was a huge learning curve and that there were some things which I might never fully understand. That would require an open mind and a willingness to let go of some of my beliefs about how the world around me worked. In a way, it was like driving to work each day; although I could not explain exactly how my car engine worked, that didn't stop me getting behind the wheel and driving. There seemed little point trying to control either the healing or its outcome. That simply wasn't for me to do. I would have to trust in this gift, even if I didn't understand it, and just let go. And really, there was no reason why I shouldn't. As amazing as all of this had been, I had never once felt afraid of this new awareness, and so far nothing bad had happened as a result of it.

I went on to ask May about the changes she saw in Fred and was delighted to hear of the progress he was making in his daily life. She reported that his confidence and his spirit had lifted and the sparkle had returned to his eyes. The entire left side of his body was gaining muscle and he was becoming stronger, so daily tasks were less of a struggle. He was dragging his leg less than before and she joked that he wouldn't be wearing through his shoe as quickly. I was thrilled about all this improvement, and in only two sessions! I wondered how much could be achieved in a few more sessions. How far could this actually go? After May had left, I was so excited by Fred's progress that the rest of the day passed quickly. As I drove home, I couldn't wait to hear what Mandy would have to say when she came for tea the next day.

Saturday afternoon could not come soon enough. It was my day off, so I busied myself with household chores to pass the morning. Mandy arrived as soon as she could escape the salon and we sat down in my kitchen for tea, cake and some interesting conversation. Over and over again, "Amazing!" was her response. First we discussed Fred's session in detail and then talked about how Lucy's feet had been healed. I described some of the healing that had taken place with other clients I had helped, being careful not to mention names or divulge anyone's personal details. Mandy was very encouraging and supportive, although she confessed she would never have believed it, had she not seen it herself. It was then that I decided not to disclose the other interesting things that had been happening. I would keep those to myself until

I understood them better and could hopefully explain them.

I continued to see Fred every Thursday evening for the next five weeks. At the end of his seventh session, while we were sat drinking our tea, Fred said he felt that he didn't need to come in anymore. He believed he could continue to implement everything he had learned so far on his own. I was convinced that Fred now understood that an awareness of our thoughts is vital to the quality of our existence. By first analysing what Fred was thinking and why, we had been able to discuss how that made him feel and from there to the physical effect it was having on his body.

I had been able to jumpstart the healing process of his physical body, but his mindset and attitude at home were the determining factors. Had he not applied to his daily life what he'd learned in our sessions, the healing energy I had given him would have only been able to get him so far; not nearly so far as his daily resolve to remain positive in thought and deed had taken him. When I first met Fred, he had had to drag himself into my salon; I have no illusions as to how disabling a stroke can be. I think the reason Fred's healing was only able to go so far was because of his age and because of how much time had passed between when his stroke occurred and when we were able to begin the healing process.

The length of time someone has lived with a disability will determine to what extent it can be reversed. But even at seventy-three years of age and after having had a stroke, Fred had managed to get his life back. After only seven sessions he was able to drive again, his confidence grew to the point that he was interested again in a social life and was able to go out with friends and meet for his beloved quiz night. He was interested once more in his hobbies and was now enjoying them with a renewed enthusiasm. His wife was able to get out of the house again because she didn't have to worry about leaving him alone anymore. No more dragging his foot around like a dead weight. The muscle wasting was reversed in both his left leg and arm and he could feel his left hand again so he was able to do more with it. There was a great change in the man who was once completely dependent on his wife, and wouldn't even leave the house.

There was no one more delighted than me to see the changes in Fred, so when he felt he didn't need any more sessions with me, I was filled with contentment and gratitude. Few things are more satisfying than the knowledge that you have helped to improve the quality of someone's life.

Unfortunately, I didn't have the opportunity to see Fred again. Not long after his last session, I moved to my new home and began healing full time. After I moved, we lost contact. I hope he is still well and still carrying with him what he learned; may God bless my friend. I will be forever grateful for the experience I had with him. Fred made me realise that there is no illness that I cannot treat with a good degree of success and I have taken that knowledge, along with the confidence it inspired in me, and applied it to the thousands of people who have sought my help. My experience with Fred confirmed that we are not alone. It had clearly taken more energy than I possessed to lift him like that!

The pictures that I had seen so clearly continued to fill my head and I sensed that it was time for me to start another drawing. This time it would be the energy circle, an amazing universal scene set in a cavity: a place of pure moving energy within itself. I could feel the energy of this second drawing and I felt that this one would be stronger than the first, but in a different way. Although I felt that I was ready, I was a little apprehensive. Until that first drawing, I had only ever drawn at school, so this promised to be interesting.

I started to get the visualisation, just like the first one and it felt so powerful that I decided to start the energy circle that night. I still had black paper and everything else that I needed from my first shopping trip. After dinner, I went straight upstairs. I was not sure how this drawing would turn out as the first one was totally different. I began by drawing a circle and then started to add colour, building it up using red, white and a small amount of blue. Just like before, my hands were moving wildly and at one stage I started to laugh. I couldn't help it; I had never seen myself as an artist but they obviously thought differently. Just as I thought I had finished, my hand moved right across the paper and destroyed the drawing, well most of it anyway. I was mortified. All you could see was a faint shading of where the drawing had been and I knew that it was not right.

I started again, focusing hard on the pictures in my mind to make sure that I had a mental framework to produce what was needed. I drew the scene exactly as I saw it in my head. This time, I had to concentrate even harder than before. I had to try to separate my conscious vision from the other drawings that I could see and focus on this particular drawing. I knew when I started this drawing that it was going to be mind boggling. The drawing is unusual but has a really nice feel to it, as if it were alive; you can almost feel the energy flowing from it. I felt that the presences were joining their energy with mine through this drawing and I knew that I would just have to wait and see what happened.

One thing that my healing has taught me is that as individuals we are all very special. Each of us is unique, and the way in which healing takes place differs from person to person. The colours that are used in healing vary for each person. As healing progresses, the colours change. Only when progress is not as expected will the same colour be needed, because the sufferer's attitude is not changing towards their illness, so the illness is still in charge, and I have to turn that around. Usually purple, a very powerful colour is used for communication. The colours that we wear can also affect us and our moods. I knew that my drawings had to reflect the effects that colours have on us as individuals and so it was important to bring in a range of colours that would address our weaknesses. By the time the drawing was finished, I looked like a clown. The bedroom looked worse than when I had done the first drawing, and that had been bad enough! I knew that I would have to find a way to overcome the mess, as I was spending more time cleaning than sleeping!

I first discovered the term 'shearing' while staying with my sister Janet. Her family used to come for Sunday lunch and the little ones would excitedly tell us all about their week and of adventures to come. One Sunday, we decided to visit my younger sister who lived about 5 miles away. As we prepared to leave, Janet turned off the gas fire and went to put her coat on. Her grandson, Daniel, was on the floor and as he started to get up, he stumbled. He put his hand out to steady himself and it landed flat against the fireplace. Daniel let out such a scream as he clenched his little hand. As his Mum ran over to him I said straight away, "Let me see. Let me take the pain away". As I did, Daniel asked me, "Do you know what you're doing?" "Well, yes I'm giving you healing," I answered. "No," he said, "It's called shearing. That's what you do; that's what God did".

All of us just looked at each other. I asked again, "What did you say Daniel?" He answered, "What God did, that's what you do". "How do you know that word?" I asked. "I don't know," he replied in a matter-of-fact way. I remembered then what it symbolised; the Lamb of God. That was what I had read in The Bible when I was a child. God, shearing, taking away. That's what I do with my clients; I take away their negative energy by using shearing and replace it with positive energy. In order to maximise the results and to aid healing, all the negative energy must be removed and the meridian lines unblocked. Any negative energy left behind will grow again.

It is also very important that clients try to minimise stress and anxiety in their lives, as emotional wellbeing has a major effect on physical health. Physical ailments are normally caused by emotional imbalances and healing can only help if the recipient is prepared to help him or herself. It is difficult to describe the weight of the responsibility that I felt while I worked on the drawings. I was very conscious of the need to get them exactly right and each drawing took me several days to achieve. It was an exhausting process and I could not have done it without the support of my family and friends. In particular, my sister Janet was wonderful; she just seemed to take it all in her stride and gave me both the space and support that I needed. I would leave early in the morning to go to the salon and no matter how late I arrived home, there would always be a meal waiting for me. I stopped seeing my friends. I just wanted to concentrate on everything that I was being taught and I knew that somehow the drawings would bring me a greater energy to work with.

When I had finished the drawings, I approached three different people about having them framed. Although each one told me they would do the job, not one of them ever came back to me and it was this that made me realise that they were not meant to be framed. By framing them, I would have prevented vital extra energy from the drawings from flowing into me and into my healing room and thus restricted my universal input. And so the drawings remained as they were.

I had helped so many people in such a short time and I had been presented with new challenges almost daily, but so far I had taken everything in my stride. In February 1996 I was approached by a member of Penarth Spiritualist Church who asked if I would consider giving healing to a lady with throat cancer. Mary was a patient at Velindre Hospital, a well-known cancer hospital in Whitchurch, Cardiff. I agreed immediately. I didn't know if I dared to think that I could make a difference to this poor lady, but I was ready to do everything I could to help her beat this terrible disease.

At this time, I was still working mornings in the salon and healing in the afternoons and so Sunday was really my only day off. I arranged to visit Mary on Sunday 4th February with her friend from the Spiritualist church. On the way to the hospital, she asked what I was going to do that first day and without thinking I told her that I was going to pull the cancer through the skin. As soon as I had said it, I realised how mad that sounded, to me as well as to her, but I knew that was exactly what I had to do.

As we drove into the car park, I saw Velindre Hospital for the first time. It wasn't at all as I had imagined: it looked rather run down and was much smaller and less imposing than I would have expected for a hospital that cared for so many people battling the most frightening of diseases. Walking through the hospital, my thoughts were on Mary and the work I was about to do. I listened very closely to the instructions that were filling my mind: it seemed that her first treatment was to be very intense. I could not imagine how it must feel to be a cancer patient, but the sense of illness, sickness and pain was palpable and I could feel it all around me. I had never experienced anything like it but I knew that I had been sent here for a purpose and so I began to prepare myself for what lay ahead.

As I approached Mary, I held out my hand to introduce myself. She was a beautiful lady with a very tired face and I sat and chatted for a while to prepare us both for her first healing treatment. With the curtains closed for privacy, I instructed the lady who had accompanied me to remain seated well away from the bed throughout the session. As I raised Mary's bed to make it easier for me to reach, I could feel the energy around her neck and told her to lie back and relax. As I held my hands just above Mary's throat without touching her skin, I felt a tremendous and immediate heat. The skin around her neck looked like it was pulsating; it was as if there were balloons under the skin which were being pumped up. Her neck was pulsating as if it was alive with an enormous energy. It was an incredible sight. Her friend stood up to look but I told her to stay back as I felt that someone else's presence would cause the energy to change. At the end of the healing session, it was a while before Mary opened her eyes, but that was not unusual. I told her to rest and not to worry about anything that might happen afterwards. She thanked me and remarked on how hot her neck had felt, which I reassured her was normal. We said our goodbyes and I told Mary that I would see her the following week.

As we left the hospital, it felt like my head was doing cartwheels. On the journey home, Mary's friend asked me about what I'd said earlier about how the cancer would come through the skin. I replied that I expected it to happen sometime that day. I sensed that she was unhappy that I had not included her in Mary's treatment and we did not talk much for the rest of the journey. When she dropped me home, she said that she would let me know if I was needed the following week. The rest of the day was spent as any other Sunday. After lunch with my sister's family, I washed up and went to my room to rest and reflect on the morning's events.

The next morning I received a phone call to tell me that within two hours of leaving the hospital Mary's skin had opened and the cancer was now lying on the outside of the throat. I knew then that her recovery had begun. Although I had told Mary that I would see her the following week, I still didn't know if I would be asked back and it wasn't until 10.30pm that Monday night that I received a phone call confirming that I was to see Mary again.

In the meantime, Mary's friend from the Spiritualist church had come to see me on the Tuesday afternoon. She said that she had just been to see Mary and that she was in a dreadful state. I told her that I knew that Mary was all right, as I had learned by then to trust my work. Throughout that week, I prepared myself for the coming Sunday, listening intently to the teachings of the spiritual world to which I now belonged and I somehow knew that I would have an even stronger power than the week before. If the cancer had come through the skin after just a few hours last time, then what would happen next? I knew that this time the healing was going to be even more focused on the huge mass that had to be dealt with.

By the time Sunday came, I felt at peace with myself and not at all nervous, although the knowledge that I had been chosen to help Mary made me feel quite humble. Her friend from the church was giving me a lift again and as we set off, I sensed that she wanted to chat. I asked if she had been back to visit Mary. She said that she hadn't, although others from the church had. I knew that she couldn't wait to know what I was going to do that day and when she asked me, I told her that I was going to burn the cancer away. She was aghast and asked how I thought I was going to do that. I replied that she would see for herself but that this time she really must stay away from the bed. She didn't say anything and the rest of the journey passed in silence.

When we arrived, Mary was lying down and the Ward Sister, who had been sat on the bed chatting to her, stood up to greet us. Before leaving, she told me that I was to ask the nurses for anything that I needed. We sat and chatted with Mary for a while and I could see for myself the difference in her neck. It was the first time that I had seen a cancer on the outside of the skin. The open wound on Mary's neck had to be protected as much as possible and so had been painted with gentian violet to prevent infection. It was a lovely shade of purple and I told her that I liked the colour. When I asked how she had been after the last session, she again remarked on the intense heat that she had felt. I asked if she was ready for me to continue and she nodded, saying that she trusted me and that I must do whatever was necessary. At that moment, I could have cried.

As I examined Mary's neck, the full extent of the cancer and the damage it had done was very apparent. I had never seen so much swelling in such a small area and the whole area was covered in what looked like peeled grapes. I had noticed quite a difference in Mary's face from the previous week and the colour of her skin was encouraging. Where the back of her neck had been purple, a more skin-like colour had developed. The skin looked a healthier, more natural colour.

Mary's friend was sat away from the bed but before I could begin, the pillows had to be arranged in the shape of the cross, with Mary's neck positioned in the centre. I was determined to reduce the swelling and dry up the affected area on the neck. I felt my hands tingling as I held them above Mary, working away I concentrated on the front and sides of the neck. As the healing progressed, the affected area began to dry and traces of salts appeared from the skin. I asked Mary's friend if she wanted to see and showed her the little grain-like specks where the cancer had been. As the skin was repairing, I kept checking with Mary to make sure that she was not in pain. I continued healing from side to side, balancing the spiritual energy that was drying the sodden skin.

When I had finished, I asked Mary to be positive and strong from now on. To help her body heal, it was important for Mary to believe that she would survive and to visualise herself in the future. Mary's bed had been lowered to make it easier for her to get in and out but this meant that she could not see out through the window. I felt that the view from the window, combined with the breeze when it was open, would help Mary to daydream and encourage her to make plans for the future.

The difference in Mary's appearance after that second session was incredible. I called her friend over to see. Mary's skin was now bronzed and glowing and most of the swelling had gone. It looked almost normal but for the presence of what looked like little dried-up currants where the grape-like clusters had dried and shrivelled. Mary could also feel the difference and she knew then that the healing was working. As we said our goodbyes, she asked me to come back the following week. I was so pleased that she had asked me herself and I agreed straight away. Walking away from the ward, I turned and saw that Mary was sat up, waving and saying goodbye. It was a wonderful sight and all the way home her friend and I talked about the healing that had taken place. Mary looked so different and it was the most humble feeling I have ever experienced.

However, despite the progress in those first two sessions, I knew that the next stage of Mary's healing would be very difficult. I felt subconsciously that it would have to be performed in a different way, using my imagination and just following my guides. I knew that I would have to keep Mary comfortable but also continue giving healing to weaken the cancer. At that point, Mary could not open her mouth very well and was being fed through a tube in her nose. I knew that, now the swelling had gone down, the next thing I had to do was to clean out Mary's throat and get it working again so that she could eat and drink normally.

I hoped that when I saw Mary next, I would see a difference in her spirits, as well as in her neck. When I arrived for her third healing session, I found that the doctors had given her a blood transfusion; three bags in total, as well as other treatment which her body was not happy with. There was nothing I could do about this, although I hoped that we would be able to work together in the future. That day was the day that I was to start work on Mary's throat and although she looked so frail that I did not want to disturb her, I knew that before I could start, I had to clear out all the mess left over from the healing that Mary had had so far.

It felt as if someone was telling me exactly what to do. I began to prepare Mary for her third treatment, moving the pillows into the right place and positioning her bed properly. Mary looked tired but I knew that she would benefit from what was about to happen. I started working around the throat area and down into the neck to clear all the mucus that had gathered there. It was almost as if I had x-ray vision! Imagine a corkscrew made of golden coloured light and with a narrow end. The narrow end was going down and as it went deeper, the end of it looked as if it was turning and gently taking something away from the sides of Mary's throat. Mary would have to bring all this mucus up but I felt that although it would be hard, she could do it. She did not make a sound as I worked, but she seemed aware of what was taking place. Although Mary was tired that day, I was sure that she was capable of dealing with the treatment and I felt that she knew what was happening without me telling her.

I felt that Mary must be an extraordinary person to allow me to do all this without even knowing me and I felt very blessed at her allowing me to experience and learn about my gift in this way. As the session ended, I remember feeling quite overwhelmed. I asked Mary if she was all right, to which she replied that she was fine, but that she had experienced some strange and interesting sensations. Then I asked if she thought that the nurses would let her have a cup of tea now that she was over the worst of it. "I would love a cup of tea," she said, "but I'm not sure". I told her that I would ask for her and that I hoped that they would take the tube out for her. I left the ward, telling her that I would see her the following week.

Throughout that week, I thought of Mary, hoping that she was making good progress and wondering if she had had her cup of tea after all. Sunday arrived and as I was on my way in to see her, I wondered what I was going to find. But I had a good feeling about the visit and as I walked upstairs to the ward, I felt my stomach doing somersaults because of the excitement. I just knew that something had happened. When I entered the ward, I could see Mary sat up in the bed, without the tube coming out of her nose. "Oh Mary, they took it out!" I cried. "Well, they had to," she said and went on to tell me exactly what had happened.

After I had left the previous Sunday, she had gone to sleep and had rested until the night. She did not know what time she had woken up but when she woke, she found that the tube was coming out of her mouth. It seemed that the tube had come up from her stomach on its own and was hanging out of her mouth. When the nurses arrived, they had to thread it back down to the stomach and then bring it out of her nose to remove it completely. The nurses told Mary that they had never seen anything like that before! Mary was able to have her first cup of tea in a very long time. I was delighted! Mary went on to tell me that she had coughed and coughed and had brought up all of the awful mucus that had needed to be released from the throat. Mary had changed beyond recognition and she looked like a different person.

CHAPTER THREE – My Guides (The Boys)

The time has come for me to tell you about my guides, or the boys, as I like to refer to them, and the work we have done together since I was first given my gift. It has been the most amazing and totally unexpected journey into the unknown and it was a great comfort for me to know that I would have company on my journey, not only in my work but in my private life as well. This chapter will hold many surprises and I will describe some of the astonishing events that took place in my new flat. That is why I have decided to introduce the boys at this point.

Although comforting, it was still a great surprise to learn that I was going to have help on the profound journey on which I had found myself. It was an even greater surprise when I realised the amount of teaching that I would receive from them, the boys; on a regular basis, they have repeatedly proven their ability to guide me in the right direction and I have followed and listened to their instructions with both interest and confidence, learning many new techniques along the way. It seems to me that healing is an unknown quantity; I have watched with interest many programmes on the subject and each time I have been disappointed by the failure to show that not every healer has their teachers to show them the way. Surely if they had, some healers would not be so aloof and reluctant to teach people how to take care of themselves?

Before I begin healing with a new client, I explain to them the involvement that the boys have. They really are the most amazing people who help and guide me in the right direction. It was very strange to find that I had the boys to help me in all aspects of my work but their guidance to put what I was doing into words has been invaluable. I understand that there are many ways that healing can be applied but the one that I have been chosen to do is shearing. We are the lambs of God and shearing means taking away - the shearing of the lambs - and it is that which I am being taught to do.

I am going to explain how all this started: the drawings that came, how the boys have taken care of me right from the beginning of this epic journey and of course the people that have come into contact with them through my work. I feel that it is important to describe the boys and acknowledge the enormity of their contribution to my work. Many clients have woken to find themselves being 'worked on' and have not been afraid to allow whatever was necessary because they can feel the difference once the boys have finished. I have stood back and watched as they have taken great care of those clients who seem to accept without question whatever takes place. Many have received regular healing at home from the boys and have asked the boys for help if they have been feeling unwell. In such instances, it has been given without hesitation and once they start to give healing, the feeling of the energy working with you is amazing. The boys are truly outstanding and they have been a big part of my life since all of this began.

They have taken the utmost care of people with whom they have come into contact. As we are all different, physical treatment is tailored to each individual but for most people this includes strengthening of the physical body. A good example of this is a lady aged over eighty who comes to me periodically and lets them loosen her limbs to help her joints cope with everyday activities. I have seen many people who have muscular problems and issues with tendons, ligaments or anything that makes movement difficult and it is quite remarkable to watch how the Boys treat them. Over the years, I have watched as many of my clients have felt the boys' hands holding and touching them. Many are taken to a different level of consciousness and several have brought their family or friends to witness what has happened. One lady in particular asked me if she could she bring her husband so that he could watch. I agreed and on the following visit, her husband accompanied her. I prepared a place for him to sit on the other side of the couch so he didn't miss anything. He sat in amazement as he watched fingerprints from invisible hands appear on his wife's skin. When incidents like this are witnessed by others, they validate the phenomena that so often occur in my work.

I have welcomed the teachings that I have had. It has been fifteen years now and it is still going strong. I am very excited about how much has been taught and the level of work that I have reached. I test myself often to make sure that I am not missing anything I could be improving on. Reconnection of meridian lines is just unbelievable, the strength that is used when the stretching movements begin. This takes place regularly to help the structural body, where maintaining the right level is vital to ensure that we are standing correctly. When this is being done, some clients end up so close to the edge of the couch that I stand up just in case they fall off! You would think by now that I would know they are all right: I do, it is just me being overly cautious and being over protective of my clients. All my clients have benefited from the boys' kindness, both at their sessions and at home, and are still benefiting today; but the time when I really needed strength was when I moved into my flat. They proved to me that I am protected. I needed to be.

The night I moved into the flat I felt a bit uneasy because of the negative energy there, which was very unusual for me, so I asked my friend Judy to stay for that first night. As I did not have much furniture, it was an easy move for me and it was nice for my sister to have her home back. She and her family had been extremely kind, letting me stay with them while my flat was being refurbished.

The lad next door lent me a two-seater settee, so Judy and I had something to sit on. We opened a bottle of wine and started a good old 'girly' chat, as best we could because of the horrendous noise that was coming from the neighbours upstairs. We could hardly hear ourselves speak but that did not seem to matter as we had not seen each other for some time.

We had a lot to talk about so we decided to go into the front room that, when finished, would eventually become my healing room. Everything else was more or less done. I had to buy some furniture, but what I did have was in the middle of the room covered over with a sheet so we could at least get around the room for painting. I had to leave it until last because I was unsure what colour I was going to use. I knew it had to be green but had yet to decide on the exact shade.

Judy loved the flat. I told her that I was glad she was there because it was a big flat and I would have felt uneasy being alone that first night, as I sensed that a lot of unpleasant things had gone on there. We went to the kitchen at the other end of the hall but the noise from upstairs was so loud that we decided to go back into my healing room. I was explaining how I hoped to finish the room and Judy was giving me some advice on where to put everything, including the couch and how the windows should be dressed. There were four long windows and the sills were quite low so Judy sat on one of them. I was talking about how the room was going to look, just girl talk, when all of a sudden she shot up, screaming and ran out of the room. She was yelling, "My back! Something is stabbing me in my back!"

I followed her down the hall, confused and worried. She kept yelling it over and over. When I caught up with her, I spun her around so I could look at her back but there was nothing there. She was saying it again and I told her, "No, there is nothing wrong with your back". "Yes there is I can feel it!" I grabbed her and held her until the feeling had passed. No sooner had it gone away, than she started describing seeing friends of my Mum who used to come and visit when we were little children. I knew she was telling me the truth because of what she was saying. She was really upset by this time and even more so because I could not see them myself.

That night, Judy saw people that had passed over some time ago. They were family friends, but she saw my Aunty Carrie in particular; I used to go and stay with her as a child and when I was older and she came to visit, I would always walk her to the bus stop. On the way home I used to love looking up at the stars. To me that was such a delight, seeing all the stars that seemed to be in one place, not thinking just how large the sky really was, but I was young and not yet wise to the world and everything in it. Even as young as three years old I would open the curtains and look up at the stars and ask whoever lived there to come and get me as I didn't like it here anymore! To this day I still love looking up at the stars in the night sky.

Seeing Judy react like that was such a shock. Finally, she started to put on her coat, ready to leave. "Please don't leave," I said. "Whatever is happening, you must tell me, because I cannot see it, only you can; please don't be scared". I was more worried about the things we could not see than the things she was seeing and I did not want to be there on my own, not after all that had happened. I was desperate for her to stay.

I loved the flat and knew it would be great for work, but it had a really funny feeling to it and I sensed I was going to have to reclaim it from whatever had taken hold of it. I knew I could make it look fabulous, so the fight was on, but what was I fighting against? If I could just stay that first night, then the first stage would be over - at least I hoped it would - but Judy was just screaming the place down. Eventually I managed to calm her. I begged her to stay, saying that I was afraid and did not want to be alone and after a while she agreed to stay.

But Judy's ordeal was not over yet. As we sat together and tried to understand what had happened and why, she suddenly stood up and said in a very matter of fact tone, "I have to wash your feet". "Don't be so silly, you're not washing my feet". "Yes, I am. I have to". We stood there arguing over her wanting to wash my feet and then she shouted, "I'm leaving then!" "Please don't go, Judy," I pleaded. "Well then, let me do it, Anne. I have to do it". I agreed reluctantly, having no other choice. "I don't have a bowl; all I've got is a mop bucket". "That will do". I went into my bedroom to get a towel and Judy was in the kitchen washing out the mop bucket and filling it with water. I really was not happy about this at all. I even started to cry, the tears just rolling down my cheeks. With everything that had happened to me, this was the first time that I had cried. I could not bear for her to wash my feet - I was mortified at the very thought of it - but she was insistent that she had to do it or else she would leave.

And so my lovely friend got down on her knees and washed my feet. Not a word was spoken; I just did not know what to say, the only thing I could do was cry. I so badly wanted to take Judy and lift her up off her knees and hold her. But I knew that would upset her and so I just let her do whatever she wanted. She lifted up my foot and placed it in the bucket and then the other one. Both my feet were in the bucket. She never made a sound. Then, one at a time, she lifted my feet out and put them on her lap and dried them. By this time I had stopped crying and just sat there. It suddenly dawned on me that the only person who had washed my feet like that was Aunty Carrie when I used to stay with her. She was the lady that Judy had seen earlier, the lady whose presence had so alarmed her.

When we were small children, Mum used to go out with Dad, so we were all sent to stay with our Aunties. As I said previously I would stay with Auntie Carrie and she would wash my feet before bed. These were special moments for me. I was only small, probably about seven. That's what it reminded me of.

After Judy had finished drying my feet, she emptied the bucket into the sink. I took another bottle of wine from the cupboard and opened it, pouring us both a glass. We sat together and talked of the event. I was so very sorry about what had happened to her that night. About an hour later, we were both emotionally exhausted and needed to sleep. Neither of us wanted to be alone, so we snuggled down into my bed and slept all night.

We woke the next morning feeling well rested. After a shower and a cup of coffee, I could tell that Judy could not wait to leave. Under the circumstances I could not blame her! I wanted to say something but did not dare in case it upset her. We hugged at the front door and she left. I never wanted to see her upset like that again. It was just too much for me. I have seen Judy many times since, but we never mentioned it again, and only once, several years later, has she come back to stay.

~~~0~~~

After a few weeks, the shock of the events of that night faded. With hindsight, it made me stronger and I know now that I will be able to deal with whatever life may throw at me in the future. But it was not until after that night that I realised just what this flat had in store for me. I knew I could deal with it, but I did wonder what was coming next. The number of events that took place after I moved in should have sent me running, but it was as if I somehow knew that I had to get rid of some unknown undesirable presences, most likely spirits that had gathered there. I had seen enough since receiving my gift for this not to worry me unduly.

I had not been in my flat for very long, so I was just getting used to living there. I had done a lot to the flat and although it was not finished, it was getting there. But the feeling of unease that I described previously was still there. I put it down to the place having being misused and uncared for.

The first thing that happened was one day when I had come home from work. I was in the kitchen as usual when suddenly I was pushed from behind by someone, or rather something? It was propelling me towards the sink. It was really rough with me and pushed me so hard that my head nearly touched the taps, as if someone was pushing me right into the sink. It took all my might to push myself back up and turn around, but of course there was no one there. I was alone in the flat.

Somehow I knew it was some sort of entity, so I just shouted, "If you touch me again, you'll have it! Keep your hands off of me!" Then for some reason I started laughing. If anyone had heard me they would have thought I was mad but it made me feel better, so I didn't really care.

The next thing was that every time I went into the bathroom, I felt as if there were spiders about, but I searched several times and could not find any. I never felt settled about it though and I knew they were there. This went on for weeks until one night I was getting ready for bed and something made me look down behind the cistern. Out of the corner of the bathroom crawled three spiders. They were the same size and colour and were identical in every way. I could not believe that there were three of them. I soon got rid of them!

A few days later, one of my friends gave me a housewarming present, a wind chime in the shape of a little house with four or five long charms hanging down. I hung it on the door frame and walked away, thinking I would find a permanent home for it later, but before I reached the end of the hall I heard a crash behind me. Startled for a moment, I turned around to find the whole thing had fallen to the floor. I thought perhaps I had not hung it securely. I walked back and picked it up, put it back together then hung it back up and walked away. As I did, it happened again, so this time I just stood in the hall and said, "You don't like it then?" It was lying on the floor, broken into bits, and even the nylon line to which the chimes were tied was broken, as if had been cut in half. I picked up all the pieces and took them to the kitchen. I think they did not want me to have anything about the house that they did not like.

Another night, there was a knock at the door and when I opened it, it was my friend Eddie. He asked if he could use my telephone because the phone box across the road was out of order. He had been out cycling but had tired and wanted to call a taxi for a ride home. Of course I agreed. He said he would be back in a few minutes as he wanted to leave his bicycle with his friend next door and pick it up in the morning. A few minutes later he returned and apologised again for needing to use my phone. I assured him it was perfectly fine and showed him to the phone, which was in the hallway.

After he had made his phone call, he walked towards me and I remember thinking that he looked really odd. He had gone very pale and had a strange expression on his face. I asked him if he was all right, but he just said that he had to go. I told him the taxi would be a few minutes, but he insisted that he had to leave immediately, that he was being told to get out of the flat. He was white with fear and in an absolute panic. He moved past me abruptly, walked out the door and turned around when he was standing on the pavement away from the front door and said, "I'm all right by here". I was confused by his reaction and I asked him if he was joking. He replied that he was very serious and that he could not stay in the flat a moment longer. Someone or something had told him that he had to get out straight away. With that, his taxi arrived and he left. I have seen him since but he seems to be very cautious around me. He says that he will never forget what happened to him and that there was something deeply disturbing in the flat.

I had to really fight to stay in that flat and I managed it for several years, although I have since moved to a house not far away. Over the past fifteen years, I have learned that there is more to life than we will ever know, but one thing I do know is that we are protected from souls that can go neither one way nor the other. There are black holes which act as soul keepers. They give the soul protection from elements that can disturb its journey through time, in the dimension in which it is travelling. The Black Hole protects you when you are sleeping, but cannot protect you from what you take into it as thoughts. Some people may experience the feeling of being in a dark tunnel and being unable to get out, like being stuck in a rut. This is because when we go to sleep with too much going on in our heads, the brain does not shut down but keeps active and prevents us from enjoying a good night's sleep. This increases the negative energy and makes matters worse and signifies that the person is stagnating within because of something that has happened to them. We all manifest negative energy to some degree, that's normal for balance, but some produce more than others. Our minds are constantly active, particularly when we are experiencing difficulty in resolving a problem. The level of anxiety - and therefore negative energy - will depend on how anxious we become and this determines how long it takes us to get out of that rut, that tunnel of darkness. To overcome this, we need to think about what is preventing us from solving the problem. Once we have worked out how to deal with the problem, the dark tunnel will not seem so bad. But it takes a lot of commitment to police your thought patterns and not think of the problem which is causing the negative energy. For example, when you wake up in the morning pretend you're going on stage; present yourself to the world the way you would like them to see you. Fresh, smart, confident and head held high. That way you will deny the negative energy its strength and weaken its power over you, and YOU will have power over it. Things can only start to improve when we work though the issues that put us in that dark place to begin with. In truth, we create our own end and our destiny but many of us do not realise it.

If we suffer with depression, it is we ourselves who have created that depression without even realising it. The end of the tunnel is always there and it is up to us whether we choose to go through it. Experiencing these upsets and difficulties makes us stronger and more determined and helps us to understand how the universe works. Most of us can describe having an experience that made us feel like we were in a tunnel at some point in our lives. Once we have experienced that tunnel, and how it feels for life to get that low, that feeling will help us to take charge and stay in control, thus limiting further damage or problems.

As individuals, we are open to many different energies. We are vulnerable and life is hard for many people, and we need to know what happens to us and why. That is why I think that we all need to know about the different elements of energy and how we all use them without even knowing. That is our backup mechanism to help us through our lives.

As I said before, we can choose which path we follow and which direction we take. That is our decision to make but sometimes we may get stuck and lose our way. Sometimes we get lost and stay lost. But when we know about these things, we can deal with them better because we know what options are open to us. We are all familiar with the saying, 'I can see the light at the end of the tunnel'. Most animals will lie low or hide away when feeling vulnerable or threatened and we are no different. It is a natural protection instinct. Many people if they feel low will go to bed, not because they are tired, but for comfort and security. They find safety and sanctuary in their own home, and why not? If we carry negativity it will carry us. Just that little chink of light can give us confidence. If we can just go towards it and experience the feeling of being nearly out of the tunnel, we begin to experience hope and each time we go out into the world it will seem easier. The older we get, the easier it becomes as we get wiser to ourselves. Most of all we get wiser to others, who helped put us in that dark place to begin with.

We must be aware of our choices and realise that we have the choice to think in the right way. If we have problems, we must try to sort them as quickly as possible. Sometimes the elements around us can be out of control and if we are suffering in any way, we leave ourselves open to harm without realising it. It is the universe's way of keeping us safe until we are able to take care of ourselves. The feeling the black hole gives us is not nice, the depression can sometimes feel really black. Most times, we will emerge unscathed but there are occasions when we never fully recover and something of ourselves is lost.

Often, we just learn to live with the pain. It does get better over time and hopefully we do not let it happen again. We all learn by our mistakes. So the next time you feel you are in a rut, take some time out and go somewhere on your own. Sitting by water is best, as the chi is at its strongest where the land meets the sea. When you look out over the water, make sure it is a panoramic view and that it gives you a feeling of space, and look at it width ways. It's a very peaceful and humbling feeling which reminds you of your smallness but also of how powerful the elements are and how much help they can give you.

All human relationships suffer from stresses and strain at some point and having a good friend to confide in is important to all of us. Ideally, we should not let people offload their negative energy onto us but sometimes it is unavoidable. It is important for us to limit the time during which we allow negative influences to a maximum of one hour and to ensure that it does not take place in our own home. If we allow negative energy into our homes, it will stay there. It will drain anyone who comes into contact with it. Children are particularly susceptible to negative energy and it is therefore very important to do everything we can to limit their exposure to it. Ideally a shower will expel negative energy, but even taking a simple walk will help clear the effect negativity has on us.

I often hear of families at war with each other. Sadly, this is not unusual and disputes can sometimes last for years, often causing great upset. It is a sad fact of life that marriages and other close relationships break down. If there is no chance of salvaging the relationship, we should try to make a break without too much hate building up. This is even more vital when there are children involved. Children suffer in silence and it can cause illness. They often withdraw into themselves, which is not good for them and blame themselves for upset within the family unit. It is very important that we talk openly with children and explain that the unhappiness is not their fault. Even very young children understand more than we realise, so we should not underestimate them or cover things up. They do listen to conversions between adults and only get angry if they find out things we should have discussed with them. The best policy when dealing with children is honesty and openness whenever possible.

We all need to learn forgiveness in our lives, even in the most difficult situations and circumstances. It will be worth it in the end. If we do not, it will eat away at us and even though we may think that we are unaffected, it will rest in our conscience and sometimes cause a negative stream of anger that may explode at any time without warning.

Negative energy is frequently the cause of illness and in women it will often manifest as breast cancer. Without exception, every woman with breast cancer who I have seen has had some sort of trauma in their lives. It can take as long as two to three years for it to come out. There is often a correlation between the need to forgive in one area and loss in another. They both produce similar feelings and should be dealt with in the same way.

In time, we can overcome the feeling of loss as we learn to live with it. Feelings of grief and upset will eventually lessen and fade as we accept that loss is inevitable. Anger is more difficult to deal with and each time we think of the anger, we relive it and it intensifies, thus taking longer to overcome. When we try to suppress anger, it uses more and more energy because it is a negative emotion. Losing someone is a poison and requires a different form of healing but anger does more damage in the long term because it is nastier. So, for the sake of our own well-being, we should learn to forgive and to be as content as we possibly can.

~~~0~~~

The decision to include the next story has been a difficult one but I think it is too important not to share. It demonstrates how easily we can fall by the wayside and lose control of our lives. The incidents that I am about to describe took place in the early days of my teachings to become a healer. I believe that they were the universe's way of protecting me by teaching me that there were things that I could do and things that I could not.

I have many different friends from all walks of life. Some are well educated and are high achievers, while others are not. Some are very wealthy and others very poor. It is my belief that, regardless of material wealth, we are all rich in our own right and that we should all have respect for one another. Our achievements come from what we want to achieve and the will and effort we put into making these achievements happen. We have to take responsibility and make choices about where our

life is going and where we want to take it.
However, when we are struggling to find our way,
or to get that all important hand up in life, it can be
very hard and sometimes we can find ourselves in
areas that are unfamiliar.

One day, I heard that a man, whose family I knew
well when I was growing up, was having a very
difficult time and that the breakup of his marriage
was imminent. I had lost touch with them over the
years as so often happens when people lead busy
lives. But the rumours that I heard disturbed me
and I was worried about him, so I made it my
business to see if I could help in any way. I
approached his parents first, telling them that I
would like to find him and to reconnect after all
these years. They spoke to me at some length and
explained that the young man was working away
and that as it was so expensive for him to come
home every weekend to his wife and children, he
thought it best to come home at the end of every
month. His journey home brought him through
Cardiff city centre, where the lure of the casinos
was such that he found it impossible to pass
without stopping. And so each month, on his way
home to see his wife and children, he would be
drawn into the casino with his month's earnings

and he would gamble through the night. By the time he emerged the following morning, there was very little left, not only of his wages, but of himself. He was so mentally and physically exhausted that he was barely able to stand up unaided. His wife and children were sat at home waiting for him and for the money to pay the bills to feed and house them. What sort of a life is that for a young family?

After I listened to their story, I was overwhelmed with empathy for all of them. I could never have imagined that something like this would happen to him. He was such a hard working person and had never done anything wrong in his life before this. But it can happen to anyone at any time. I arranged to see him, just for a chat and uncertain of how receptive he would be. I had not finished preparing my healing room at the flat, so I knew that if he agreed to a healing session, I would have to improvise. I was not even sure that he would show up, so when he knocked on my door, I was so relieved. We sat in my sitting room and had a long chat about how he had got involved with gambling and the help that he had sought for his addiction. He clearly recognised that he had a problem and asked for my help.

As the healing room was not yet ready, the best alternative was to use my sitting room. I held my hand above his head and he closed his eyes. Almost immediately he said that he could see colours swirling around like a kaleidoscope. After about a half an hour, I had a strong urge to pull hard and as I did so, a large quantity of a black smoky substance started to come out from his body. He opened his eyes in panic, asking what on earth was happening to him. I told him to stay calm, but I knew that I was way out of my depth. Since receiving my gift, I had witnessed some amazing things but I had never seen anything like this before. Whatever it was, it kept coming out of his body as I kept pulling at it. He began to scream, "I can feel it! What the hell is it?" I told him to hold on and finally it was all released from his body. By this time he was standing. As the thick black smoke left his body, it went straight past me and disappeared. Shocked and exhausted, he collapsed in a heap on the floor.

He sobbed like a baby and was hyperventilating, so I held him in my arms and rocked him gently for ages, speaking very quietly to soothe him. It must have taken an hour or more but I did not stop until his breathing began to settle down and his sobbing subsided into just tears. His face and shirt were wet from tears and sweat and the heat radiating from him had made me sweat. We were both as wet as if we had just stepped out of a shower.

As we sat there on the floor, completely spent, I kept going over and over in my head what had just happened. It was almost too much for me to accept and I found myself trying to rationalise it, wondering if I had imagined it until he said, "Did you see that black stuff coming out of me?" I knew then that it had really happened and I replied that I had indeed seen it. We discussed how we both felt and agreed that neither of us had ever seen anything like it before. We must have sat on the floor for a long time before either of us could find the strength to move. I was exhausted and just wanted to rest and the young man left soon after, promising to ring me.

It was not until later that evening that I had the energy to shower. I remember thinking that I did not want to do another healing session on anyone ever again. After a few days my energy returned to normal but I could not stop thinking about what I had experienced with that young man. I really wanted to know how he was doing but I was reluctant to call him. That healing session was still very fresh in my mind. With hindsight, I realise what a lesson it was. I can see that I was being taught about the dark side on this particular occasion. I needed to see both sides in order to fully comprehend the power of what I was dealing with. I could not afford to have a skewed perception that would inevitably come with having only experienced the beautiful, light energy. There is also a very ugly, dark energy as well and we must all be aware of it. I suppose I had to learn about this dark energy to be able to do my job properly and stay safe.

As a result of this experience, I now understand what can happen if we lose sight of our beliefs, our standards and our morals. We become vulnerable to negative forces and energies and if we choose to follow a path that leads us into unhealthy circumstances, we are effectively giving permission to the negative to come in and control our lives. This occurs everywhere: in all walks of life, in all ages and in all income brackets. Negativity does not discriminate.

Jealousy is one form of negative energy. We all have the same chances to achieve. How and what we achieve is ultimately up to us and no-one else. I have often been asked why some people obtain more than others and my reply is always the same: "Why would you worry about what other people have?". Jealousy distracts our focus from ourselves. Instead of being envious of what other people have, we should recognise our own advantages and focus on improving our circumstances if we are so inclined.

The young man hoped to win a lot of money to take home to his wife, but what he did not see was that he already had a lot of money, his wages from work. All he needed to do was to take it home, but he was not satisfied with his lot and wanted more. He lost his way and it became an illness with him. There are many people in this world just like him. They have to have more. Conversely, there are many people who have very little of material value yet they are content. In some ways, they are the richest because they have nothing to lose.

A few months later, another very disturbing incident occurred. Although very different from the first time, it was still alarming and reinforced to me that this sort of energy can exist and interrupt a person's well-being. On this occasion, the dark energy did not show itself as it had the first time around, but it was much bigger and stronger. Mindful of this, I did not try and remove it, as to do so would have required skills that I did not yet have. But I wanted to know what energy like this was like - and I knew the boys were with me and would always take care of me.

I had made an appointment with a new client, although I was not convinced that he really wanted to be helped due to the lifestyle that he had chosen. I was still willing to help him in any way I could. As I have already said my healing room was still not finished, so I decided to use my sitting room. It contained a big settee, which was perfect for what I required. I wish that his healing session had turned out better for him, but the events that took place were very unusual and I had not experienced anything like this before.

I have always said to the boys that I wanted to see the different ways of healing, but my experiences with this gentleman and the young man who gambled nearly put me off healing for good. We began the session with a chat, as this helps me to find out exactly what has been going on and determine how I can help. The man complained of stomach pain and an abnormal feeling around his midsection. He lay on my settee and as I held my hands over his abdomen, I felt a lot of heat radiating from him, as if I were standing next to a radiator. I had experienced this sort of condensed energy before, which occurs when negative energy is at its highest and is focused on one of our weakest points. In his case, it was in his abdomen, which has strong links to our emotions. That told me that there was different energy being produced. Depending on which side of the body is most affected, i.e. right or left, I can determine whether the source of the negativity is male or female.

I could feel the area that I needed to work on but started to feel a bit anxious, which is most unusual for me. Tentatively, I began to pull my hand away from his abdomen in a shearing motion, just to see if he felt any sensation. If the energy follows my hand, then it is loose enough for me to start. I could tell from the look on his face that he felt a pulling sensation and so I continued, a little harder this time. His expression told me that he found it uncomfortable. I was taking my time because of the effect the shearing had on him and because I wanted to be sure what I was taking on. At this point I remembered what had happened with the gambler and I was concerned that it might happen again. The man looked terrified and asked me to stop. He said it felt as if I was pulling him off the settee, but I was not actually touching him. It was just the effect of me moving my hands away from him. That is how it works. My hands are a magnet to negative energy. If I move my hands away, it will follow them and that is what he was experiencing.

We were stopping and starting all the time, just so I could keep control of the situation. By this time his face told me everything, so we waited for a while until he was calm enough for me to continue. I asked if he had felt any pain, to which he replied that he had not but repeated that he had felt that I was pulling him off the settee. He also said that his stomach felt freer than before. I knew from this that it was making a difference, but no-one had ever said that they had felt their body being physically moved during the shearing process. Normally, the sensation is confined just to the area from where I am taking negative energy, not the whole body. For his whole body to feel as if it was moving told me that something was not right but I did not want to alarm him, so I said nothing. He pleaded with me to continue. The sensation seemed to be stronger when I used my left hand and I could feel the heat from way above.

By this time I knew that something was not right but I did not want to stop. The further I went into the energy, the hotter it got but I just kept going until I got to the stage of pulling the negative out. It was so powerful I did not recognise this type of energy and knew it was not going to let go! I put my hand into the position and just pulled with all I had. I could feel the energy trying to pull my hand back. The man was shouting and then his shouting developed into screaming, "It's clawing me!" It still would not let go. My hand was burning and it felt as if someone or something had scratched me, and it had. I had to let go. I just could not stand the burning sensation right across the palm of my hand. The man was still lying on the settee, curled up in a ball. I told him that the energy was too strong for me to remove and he replied that he had felt it trying to hold on to him.

I explained that because it was in the stomach area, it meant that he had taken on deep emotional negative energy and that he must have been in a very bad place in his life for this to have occurred. That type of energy can only get into the system when we are very frightened and vulnerable and it is not easily released. We all have the power to choose how we want our lives to be, but sometimes we can find ourselves in situations that we cannot control or get out of.

If we allow someone to abuse us or we live in fear of abuse, we are left unguarded because all our positive energy has run out and we have no defence. This is why people who are the victims of abuse do not know how to stop it. It is because they cannot think properly. Their body and mind think only of how to survive; they forget that they can walk out at any time. Until we start to take charge of the events that have taken place, and start to rebuild our positive energy, there will be no improvement.

I am certain that this man had been in this position. He may not have wanted to tell anyone but I sensed that something really bad had happened to him. We sat and talked for ages about the events that day and I know he left with more answers than he was expecting and also a realisation that he needed to change his lifestyle. I hope that he has been able to regain control of his life and that the dark energy will have become less strong. In time, it is possible to get rid of it altogether but it takes commitment to take care of oneself and mean it. By building our confidence and working with our inner self, we can help build awareness of the people that we are, not the people that we have become.

I will end this chapter by describing the drawing that I have made of the boys. It comprises a group of eight silhouetted figures, all standing together but each very different. You can tell by their stance that the group includes both males and females. Because of some of the things that have already taken place, I believe some of the figures to be doctors and surgeons. I know that there is more to come in the drawing of the boys as I have noticed a lot more activity around them which I have not yet drawn. There may even be new people to add to the group or they may just be standing in preparation for new things to come.

CHAPTER FOUR
The Father, Son and Holy Ghost

One of the first things I was taught during my healing journey is that the solar plexus area is the most sensitive part of the body and plays a major part in our well-being. To keep the body working well, energy has to flow through this area to help maintain circulation and keep the meridian lines clear.

When everything is functioning correctly, this area can also affect our emotional state of mind. The Chinese introduced acupuncture to unblock meridian lines. I use shearing to do the same job. Shearing was one of the first techniques shown to me and it has been invaluable. It has made such a difference to so many people and has helped to relieve and even eliminate long standing illnesses. Shearing can also help to reduce swelling and lessen the symptoms of destructive and degenerative illnesses. The only side effect that I have found is that, when I use the technique frequently, it builds large muscles in my arms!

I often encourage clients to bring a friend or relative with them when having healing as this allows people to see my work for themselves. It provides confirmation that healing can work and it is human nature for people to seek that confirmation.

When my journey began, I was very sceptical about the whole thing and I needed to see everything for myself. My work has proved to be such a learning curve. The way in which I communicate with the boys changes for each client, as this allows me to work with each individual person's energy levels. I receive information on how to treat each client as a thought pattern - try to imagine having a conversation with someone simply by thought transmission and you'll have some idea of how extraordinary this is.

As individuals, we are all affected by others in positive and negative ways. When the influence is negative, this can weaken us both physically and mentally. People of all ages are affected and when the negative influence dominates a particular area of our lives, we can lose our direction. The atmosphere around us can interfere with our energy as well. We each have built in mechanisms that can support and help us to recover using the thought pattern that is right for us. When I am working on a client, I can sense if they are experiencing difficulty in getting themselves back on track. Negative energy can be a long term problem and overcoming it requires real commitment and self belief, especially when it has been there for a long time. Over time, it can accumulate and gain power, but it is still possible for us to overcome it by changing our thought patterns. It is us alone that govern how our minds think and once we realise that, we can choose to change how we think at any time by bringing our minds to a more controllable area of awareness. Many of us do not realise that we are capable of such awareness and that as human beings we have the most extraordinary abilities.

~~~0~~~

I was moving on to another level of awareness and I was apprehensive about it. I was also conscious that I did not want to miss any of this particular area of learning about the mind. I expect this to be a lifetime of unbelievable teachings and I will endeavour to pass them on to as many people as possible, to help sustain them through the journey of life. I felt a mixture of awe and total disbelief at what was happening to me. I can constantly hear the boys telling me the same thing over and over: "You can do surgery". Surely I had misheard them. I had been taught to do many extraordinary things, but surgery? That was another matter entirely. I stood in the bathroom, applying my make up, and wondered if such a thing was really possible.

My friend Pat, who came once a week to help me keep the flat clean and tidy, was vacuuming the carpet in the healing room. As I walked in, she turned to me and said, "You can practice on me if you want to". I looked at her in amazement - what had she just said? How could she have known? I asked her what she meant. "I don't know," she replied, "it just came to me as you walked in. I've got a bad shoulder, so practice on me. Have a go, Anne. You don't know what you can do until you try".

So Pat lay on the couch and I put my hand over her shoulder to start. She felt everything and described all the feelings to me as I worked. After that session, Pat's shoulder went from strength to strength and soon recovered completely. It was quite incredible and she was absolutely thrilled.

All day I thought about the different ways in which this new technique could be used and wondered when I would next have the opportunity to try out my new gift. I knew when a lady with a stomach ulcer rang me that the time had come. She had been ill for months and was in a great deal of pain. When the stomach area is blocked, it can cause nausea, which in turn can cause severe headaches. The client lived locally, so it was easy for her to get to me. It took about seven visits until doctors confirmed that the ulcer had gone. That is how I found myself on the road to surgery. As a person, I have a tendency to be self-critical and I demand a lot from myself. It has taken many years and a lot of hard work to master this technique but I have never looked back.

With some clients, however, I find that no matter how hard I try, I just cannot get it right. As long as I know that I have done my best for them, I am satisfied. The client's emotional state of mind plays a huge part in the extent of their recovery. There are some people who seem content to suffer - it is almost as if they enjoy ill-health and do not want to get better. When I was working in the salon, I treated a lady who had a bad knee. From the very first session, she was convinced that I would not be able to help her. When her knee started to improve, she told me that she would not be coming back as if her knee recovered, she would lose her benefit and have to get a job. I stood there aghast, my mouth opened in shock, as she got up, said goodbye and left!

I found it absolutely incredible that she would rather be ill than be well enough to be able to return to work, but I have since found that there are many like her. Our emotional state of mind plays a huge part in our well-being and, depending on what we want from life, its influence can be positive or negative. I did not know at first how important this would be in my work, but I began to realise as I was being shown how to unblock meridian lines. Negative thinking affects the body's balance and personal problems can easily manifest into a deep emotional trauma. Often when a client comes to see me for the first time, they complain of a physical ailment, but in time it becomes apparent that the root of the problem is emotional. The longer it takes to sort out a problem, the harder it becomes to get rid of the negative energy. Emotional issues often manifest as problems in the bowel area. If this area of the body struggles to perform, it means that our emotional overload is causing the body's waste to stay in the intestines for too long. This can cause constipation, which can be very uncomfortable and cause headaches, nausea, hot flushes and bloating around the waist. In turn, constipation can result in stagnation in other areas of our lives. I often think that if people told their doctors about the personal problems that they are experiencing, it would save a lot of time. I believe it is important to explain this in detail because this area of the body is the most verbal for all of us. If we take more care of our emotional well-being, our physical health will benefit.

Often though, the emotional damage begins when we are children. Children's reactions to what happens around them can sometimes be very limited as they assume that their experiences are normal. For example, if children come from a violent family they often assume that other families are the same. But children's failure to react visibly does not mean that they are unaffected. Anal retention and constipation is quite common in children, as letting go of things can be very difficult, especially if there is a lot going on around them. Children who experience emotional trauma often turn out to be emotionally vulnerable adults. As we grow up, we have more opportunities to help ourselves but sadly many still suffer in silence. My work has brought me into contact with many people who are still trying to come to terms with the way in which their parents treated them. Smacking used to be an accepted form of punishment but for some children, it went far beyond an occasional smack on the legs or bottom.

Many others suffered years of sexual abuse, some from an early age. I have heard the most horrendous stories of cruelty inflicted on children who had no-one to turn to for help. Many of those children are still dealing with the terrible legacy of years of abuse. Sadly, it is no less common today and all too often we hear reports in the media of babies and children being beaten or starved to death by their parents or other family members.

Abuse at any age is unforgivable but the lasting effect on children can be totally devastating. They often suffer in silence, acting as if nothing has happened. I call it silent emotion. The long-term effects are often not seen until they become parents themselves, when all too often the victim becomes the abuser and the whole cycle of abuse begins over again.

When victims of abuse reach adolescence, they often need professional help to deal with all the memories and emotions that come flooding back. The reason that these memories and emotions return in adolescence is that as children we adapt to our surroundings and reaction to trauma is often delayed until we are much older. The problems wait deep in our sub-consciousness until we are mature enough to deal with them. But they can still cause damage and affect our day to day behaviour without us being aware. When abuse continues into the teenage years and beyond, the damage can be irreparable and can destroy the victim's ability to integrate into society.

Playing is vital in allowing children to develop their inner selves. Society inevitably seeks to impose its own expectations of how individuals should think and act, and most of us subconsciously want to conform to society's view of what is normal. But as humans we are all different and should be allowed to take our own path as our life develops.

The first step in a child's integration into society is through school. This is usually the first time that the child comes into contact with people, other than their immediate families, whose role it is to guide them and put them on the right path. With the right support from parents, family and teachers, children can be guided in the right direction and encouraged to develop the skills they will need for the future. The seeds sown at this early stage will play a significant part in the child's development into adulthood.

While positive influences help to shape a child into a rounded and well-balanced individual, negative influences can have exactly the opposite effect. One of my former clients remains so traumatised from childhood that, at the age of thirty five, he had to mentally take control and prepare himself for work each morning. The pattern of abuse from his childhood continued into his adult life and it seemed that each day he would wait for the inevitability that his manager would find some reason to pick on him. Eventually the situation became so bad that he decided to leave his job and become self employed, thus removing himself from the environment in which the abuse could take place. In doing so, he allowed himself to build up his self esteem and although it took a considerable length of time, he now runs a successful business working for himself and no longer feels intimidated by others. He is finally in control of his life and has begun to recover from the abuse that he suffered as a small boy.

In my work, I hear so many stories of adults abused as children that I believe I have come to understand why society does not function properly. How can it, when so many adults had such a bad time as children? So many people suffer emotional trauma which then causes symptoms in the solar plexus area. To overcome this, we have to find the strength to deal with the situation that caused the trauma. It is possible to achieve this by monitoring and regulating the amount of time for which we allow ourselves to think about the most prominent memories. I recommend allowing no more than an hour at first and gradually increasing this, concentrating on those memories and details that are foremost in our minds. The mind is being fed from the consciousness, where all our memories are stored, and the information that comes most readily to mind is often the starting point of what is causing the problem. If we can identify this starting point and allow ourselves to think about it in a controlled way for a limited period of time, then we can begin to take control. In doing this, we can reduce the influence of the original trauma on our lives and it will become less of a problem. Although it will never completely disappear, the pain will diminish if we do not allow it to intimidate us any longer. For many, it can take years before they are able to come to terms with the past, but when we understand what we are feeling and why, it is much easier to achieve.

But it is not just children who are victims of abuse. Some of the worst incidents of abuse involving adults seem to occur in the workplace, usually among office staff. Many of my clients have experienced verbal abuse and bullying in the workplace, often by managers, and most are unable to stop it unless they find another job and leave. People who are subjected to bullying in the workplace frequently suffer with stress and other emotional problems. Likewise, many teenagers and adolescents experience bullying, especially when starting secondary school. Parents are often completely unaware that their child is having problems in school, as older children are less likely to tell them that something is wrong and usually suffer in silence or try to resolve matters themselves.

Suppressing our true feelings can be very damaging and letting go of emotion and negative energy is important. But not everyone is able to do this and unfortunately some people reach a stage where they cannot see a way out. Sometimes they make the ultimate sacrifice, like the next person who I will describe.

Richard felt that the problems in his life had become too much for him to bear and he no longer wanted to live. He was a very handsome young man and a beautiful person. He was so well loved; everyone who knew him loved him and if he had only known that, I feel certain that he would have given himself just a little more time. When I think of him today, I wish that I had known then what I know now. I feel privileged to have known Richard and I will never forget him.

His death was a great loss to the local community. His family is well-known in Penarth and I knew them personally. Through my work as a hairdresser, I got to know many local people but Richard was different to most. He was always very particular about his hair and would have it cut every three weeks and sometimes more often if there was a special event. He was fun-loving and worked very hard. Richard was at his happiest when he was working. I first met him when I worked at the hairdressers at the end of the street were Richard lived. It was a busy salon and Richard was a regular customer. When I left to manage another local salon, many of my clients followed me, including Richard. He continued to come in regularly, but not as often as previously. One day he came to have his hair cut but he did not seem himself. He had lost his job and despite all his efforts, he still could not get work. That was the last time I ever saw Richard alive. All he had wanted was to find a job to support his family but his failure to find work was just too much for him to cope with and tragically Richard took his own life. The whole town was devastated by this tragic loss.

When I began my healing work, I had no idea of what to expect but a lot of the healing that I find myself doing is beyond anything that I could ever have imagined. Being asked to help families facing life and death situations has been humbling and there has been much more for me to learn than I would have expected. The calmness with which I have been able to approach even the most challenging of situations has taken me completely by surprise. I have often been asked to visit people in hospital and I always do whatever I can to help.

On one occasion, I was approached by a family who had been given the devastating news that their son was brain dead following a tragic accident. They were absolutely desperate and were prepared to try anything. This story changed my whole view of life. I learned so much from this young man, whose name was Darren, and I think his story will help to give the reader a better understanding of what happens when we die; to understand that we do not just die but that our loved ones are still around us and that we will see them again when it is time for us all to return home.

One morning, in the early hours, my daughter phoned to ask for my help for one of her friends. She picked me up and drove me to the hospital, where I was shown to the young man's bedside. His family told me what had happened. Darren was a handsome young man of twenty three, with all his life ahead of him. He and his fiancée had been enjoying a few drinks during a night out with friends, laughing and joking, when Darren fell over hitting the back of his head. His friends, still laughing, helped him up. Darren was a bit wobbly on his feet and he and his fiancée decided to call it a night. When they got home, Darren was still wobbly but they attributed this to the alcohol and went to bed.

The next morning, his fiancée got up first and then tried to wake Darren, who seemed to be in a deep sleep. She tried everything to wake him but soon realised that something was wrong and called an ambulance. When they arrived at the hospital, the full extent of his injuries became apparent and his family were summoned. Throughout that day, tests were carried out but late evening they were given the news that Darren was brain dead and there was nothing that could be done for him. My daughter was one of the friends with whom Darren and his fiancée had spent the previous evening when Darren had fallen over.

I have never been able to understand why young people need to be taken at such a young age; I suppose it must just be the way it is. Darren must have been so special for his life to have been cut short in such a tragic way. His fiancée told me that he loved life and was such fun to be with and that just being in the same room with him would make you smile.

The situation at the hospital was so delicate. I could not begin to imagine what that family must be going through; their world was falling down around them. Losing someone so young places such a strain on family and friends and I did not know how to handle the situation. At one point I really felt that I could not stay, as I knew that there was nothing I could do for Darren. But what took place that night was one of the most unbelievable events that I have ever experienced. I realise now that I was there to learn a major lesson about our human make-up. I was there to pass on this knowledge of life to others and to comfort and reassure Darren's family.

Darren's head was so badly injured. It was a devastating situation and there was I, right in the middle of it, knowing that there was nothing I could do to help. I was asked to sit at his bedside and to help in any way I could. At first glance, he looked as if he was just asleep, as if nothing was wrong with him. I sat on the left side of his bed with my hand on his and waited for the boys to give me instructions. My mind was very active which was unusual in a situation like this but I knew that it was because I was ready to be guided through what I was there to do. The boys were telling me that I had to find Darren's consciousness and it took a while for me to adjust to the area of consciousness that he was in.

Our dimensions are determined by universal energy and before I could connect with him, I had to find where he was within that dimension. As I began, I felt totally out of my depth although I had an overwhelming feeling that Darren was helping me. After a few minutes, I began to visualise him alive and going about his normal daily routine. I sat for a while just watching the pictures in my head but I said nothing to his family at this point. As I continued to watch, I saw Darren visiting his favourite places and saying goodbye. I caught up with him at his place of work and it was then that I decided to tell the family. They stared at me in silence as they waited to hear what I would say next. I began to describe what I was seeing: Darren, wearing a cream sweatshirt, in a room with bright lights set into a ceiling. The family recognised my description of Darren's workplace.

As I concentrated harder, I saw him on a family holiday and I described a fountain and green light. Darren's family seemed familiar with what I described and everyone joined in the discussion. They seemed to find comfort in remembering the places that had been part of his life. It was as if he was visiting his life to say goodbye.

The next picture that came to me was Darren wearing a dark coloured jacket with the collar up, standing next to a light coloured car. The car was an old Ford Escort and it was light blue in colour, but very pale. As I described the picture to the family again, they recognised the scene that I described. It takes time and patience to help in this way when things are at their worst and I wanted to take my time as I helped Darren's family to reflect on the very special life that God had chosen to take so young.

Next, I saw Darren with Liz, his fiancée, standing together as one. They were standing in front of apples, like Adam and Eve, and there were stacks of boxes all around them. As I described the picture, Liz recognised a place that they had visited only three weeks earlier. Darren was back to where he had enjoyed the time and surroundings, as if he wanted to see it again and experience for one final time the moments he had spent there with the one he loved. Then I saw Darren outside the home he had shared with Liz. There were big, dark doors which looked like carriage doors, either black or dark grey. His family recognised my description of the doors on the street where he and Liz had lived. He went home to say goodbye. He travelled to different places in his life to say goodbye to the things he had enjoyed.

Darren taught me so much. Through him, I learnt that the conscious can leave the body, visit places that it knows and return to past experiences that hold special memories. In his final moments, Darren was able to comfort his family with the knowledge that he was fine and was going back to where he had come from. He shared a very special time of his life with me and I feel very honoured to have been able to help and give his family the time that Darren wanted to share with them. He trusted me to reassure his family that he would always be able to visit the places that he loved and that they would be able to sense when he was near. As Darren prepared for the journey to his new life, he left his memories to those who had known him and shared his life. I sensed that his family found comfort in the pictures that I described and the fond memories they evoked.

I will always be grateful to Darren for the knowledge that he has given me and for allowing me to share the last moments of his life. It was his way of telling his family that he was all right and helping them to understand that he was not gone, but just in another place and was still able to communicate with them. I will use the knowledge that he gave me wisely and with thoughts of him and what he taught me.

It took me several days to understand and accept what had happened at Darren's bedside. I had never experienced anything like it before or witnessed the sort of trauma that his family were going though. I knew that it was time for me to start yet another drawing. I sensed that somehow this drawing had had to wait until after Darren's tragic death before being shown to me.

Although the picture in my head was of a single person, with other energies attached to it, I felt that it had to be drawn as three figures in one drawing because of the nature of what it represents and the energy that it has. I believe it to be the Father, the Son and the Holy Ghost. It is a very unusual drawing and is very spiritual. There is a general consensus that the energy coming from the drawing is freezing cold. It draws people's attention and seems to have the most remarkable effects, as on several occasions people have actually fallen asleep while standing under the drawing. For safety reasons, I have guided them, still asleep, to a chair where they have slept for up to twenty minutes. Bizarrely, on waking, some people have said that they heard me speaking in a foreign language! Reassuringly for me, this most strange phenomenon has often been witnessed by others.

The Presence
148

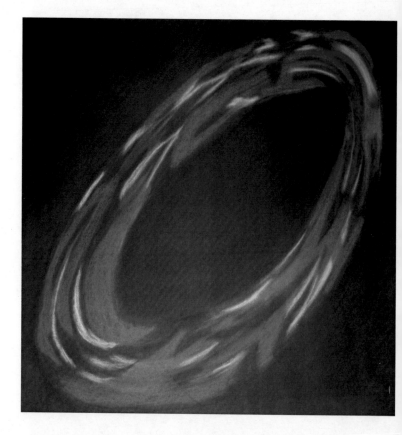

The Energy Circle

The Boys

The Father, Son and Holy Ghost

The Family

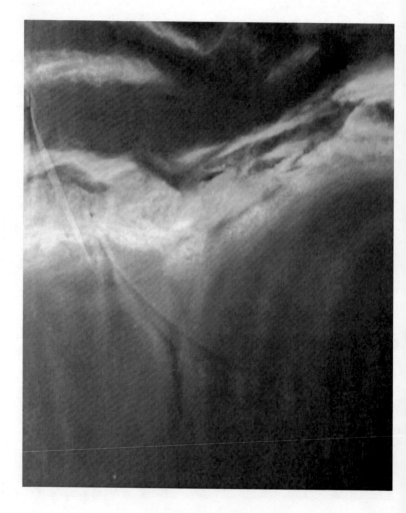

The Elements

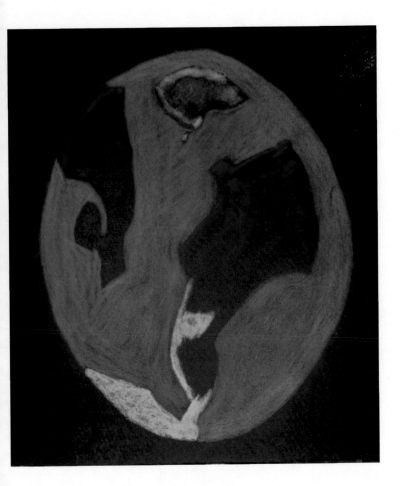

The Map

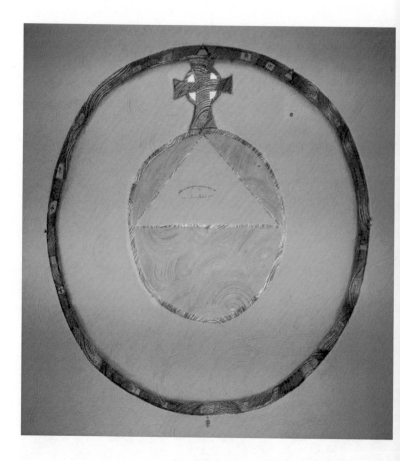

Unknown

CHAPTER FIVE – The Family

My transition from hairdresser to healer was far from easy and I can imagine how difficult it must have been for those who knew me as a hairdresser to comprehend what I was now doing. One of my most trusted clients wanted her son to see me but he refused, saying that I should stick to cutting his hair. Nathan's foot was very swollen, like a rugby ball, and he could hardly walk. The arch of his foot had dropped so much that the muscle needed to be put back into the correct position. It seemed likely that he would need an operation if he was to walk properly again. Nathan was understandably sceptical about my healing and it was only constant nagging from his mother and sister, and the prospect of surgery that finally persuaded him to see me.

To make sure that Nathan kept his appointment, his mother and sister came with him. His mother, Joanne, was one of my longest standing clients and had become a friend, so I really wanted to do a good job. Nathan lay on the couch, with Joanne sat on one side and his sister Emma on the other. I stood at the bottom of the couch and explained that

I wanted to have a good look before I started, as I like to get a feel for what is needed.

Upon examination, the arch of Nathan's right foot was chapped, indicating that the swelling was very severe. The skin looked extremely tight and its texture and colour resembled a burn. His foot was disfigured; its shape was somewhere between a rugby ball and a football, with his toes sticking out at the end. He was clearly in agony and terrified that I was going to touch his foot, but I reassured him that I was just going to reduce the swelling. I gently placed my hand above his foot so that he could experience how the treatment would feel but he shouted out and so I stopped straight away. I tried to reassure him but he said that I must have done something because he had felt it. Although he admitted that it had not hurt, he was convinced that I had touched him, despite Joanne and Emma assuring him that I had not. His reaction amused his mother and sister and because Joanne has such an infectious laugh, it was not long before we were all laughing.

Every now and then Nathan would jump, not because it hurt but because of the sensations and feelings that he was experiencing. When I got to the stage where I was ready to start pulling the swelling out, Joanne and Emma moved to the top of the couch. The shearing reduces the swelling but a lot of energy and strength is needed to remove it, and because there was so much which needed to be removed, it was going to take longer than usual. Nathan seemed happy to let me carry on, as he knew by now that I was not going to hurt him. Reducing swelling is a very interesting part of healing, as you can actually see it going down. This applies to any type of swelling. There was no need to look for the heat though, as I would normally, because the swelling was already producing heat. All I was doing was drawing that heat towards my hands. The further away I take my hands, the more of the heat comes out, so the swelling will go down, but you have to do it gently. You must not pull too fast but very slowly, to soften the area.

After about an hour, I took my hands away to check the progress; Nathan's foot was starting to take on a better shape and he seemed much more comfortable. The swelling had gone right down and slowly the arch of the foot started to reappear, allowing him to move his toes again. Everyone was delighted and a bit shocked but we had seen a significant change in Nathan's foot in a relatively short space of time. We were all delighted with the progress.

The hardest part was done; Nathan could now move his foot and wiggle his toes and he was delighted with his treatment. At first, he still experienced tightness in his foot when he walked, but that was only to be expected after such severe swelling because his tendons and ligaments had been restricted. He did not need an operation after all and it was not long before he started walking without any pain, although the stiffness would take longer to go. I did not need to see Nathan again but I would like to thank him for trusting me.

While I was still working in the salon, a woman brought her young son to see me. He looked very unwell. When I asked them to come upstairs, she carried him, which I thought was unusual because children were usually fascinated by the spiral staircase and loved to walk up and down it. She began to tell me about her little boy and when she had finished I sat there for a moment. I knew that treating him would be a huge undertaking but I was not about to turn them away. The little boy had been very sick with chronic asthma and had been admitted to hospital over thirty six times in his short life. I had no idea whether my healing would help but I knew I had to try.

With children, the healing powers that I have work very quickly, so they do not need as much treatment as adult clients and the sessions are usually much shorter. This is because children do not have the same problems that adults often have and do not usually concern themselves with trying to understand how it all works. So the little boy's first treatment was very quick, about fifteen minutes in all. Remember that this little boy was carried up the stairs because of his asthma.

I wanted to see this little boy at least twice a week, so that he would have a good chance of recovery. After the first visit, I was not sure that it had had any effect and so I was anxious to see him for a second session. When he arrived, I was just finishing a client's hair. I had decided that it would be better for me to see him in the morning. That way, he would have the rest of the day for it to work and I could send him healing all that day without him actually being present. I hoped that there had been some improvement in his condition but I certainly did not expect the overwhelming news that his mother gave me when they arrived. His mother had seen such an improvement in her son that she had decided to reduce his medication to almost half of that prescribed. I could see the difference straight away when he came in but I was alarmed that she had stopped any of his medication without his doctor's knowledge and consent. At no time have I, or would I, ask any parent to stop giving their child their prescribed medication. This was a decision that his mum had made herself because she could see how much better her little boy was. And it was truly phenomenal; he seemed to have got better almost overnight.

It was during his second healing visit that I asked his mother to start using coloured jumpers on him every day. For instance, a yellow jumper in the morning would help with circulation to improve and aid his energy levels. Alternately, in the afternoon, if he was tired, she could put a red jumper on him for a short while but not too long, because if she left it on him till late in the day he would have problems sleeping that night. The colour blue helps with bone and body structure, so it would be beneficial to dress him in that colour during the daytime. Blue also helps with aches and pains throughout the body, gives the muscles strength and helps to restructure the tubes leading to the lungs so they can open properly.

My original intention for the second session had been to remove any congestion, but his progress was so encouraging that I decided upon a completely different treatment. For some reason, I had an overwhelming urge that this little boy needed to play football. I knew just how ridiculous that sounded and so I asked myself silently if this was some sort of joke. But it was no joke; in my mind, I heard them say loud and clear, "Yes, football!" And so I asked his mother to take him out into the field and play football with him; I could scarcely believe it myself. My guides also told me that he had to be wearing a green jumper.

Green is made up of yellow and blue; green is for the heart, so with the mixture of colours it was perfect, a good all rounder, especially for something so important to this sort of exercise. It would help circulate energy flow and provide structure for playing. This little boy had not played anything physically active before because of his chronic asthma but now he went from strength to strength. Whatever had happened to the little boy who had had to be carried up the stairs only a few days ago was such a miracle. Everyone who saw him could see his transformation. When it was time for his third visit, the girls in the salon were eager to see him. After the session, his mother told them all about her son and how he had recovered.

By now, everyone had grown very fond of that little boy. When he came into the salon for his next session, it was unbelievable - he went straight to the stairs and climbed them on his own without any problems at all. His mother told me that he had not had any further asthma attacks since his last session. She had taken him to see his doctor so that he could see for himself the dramatic improvement in her son's condition and told him about his sessions with me. She had also told the doctor that she had decided not to give her son any more medication but she wanted the doctor to see and examine him first. I imagine that the doctor did not know what to think but there was no denying that the little boy's health had improved beyond belief.

The improvement was so great that after his fourth and final session, I felt that he did not need any more healing. I decided that I would keep an eye on him for a few weeks longer to be certain but he never needed my help again. I am delighted to hear that he has not needed any medication whatsoever since his healing.

~~~0~~~

I love my work and it is a privilege to be able to help each and every one of my clients, but there is one thing which gives me more satisfaction than any other - the birth of a baby. Over the years, many women have come to see me with all sorts of fertility and pregnancy problems and I have been able to help most of them. I always smile when I hear that a baby has been born to one of these women.

Three of the women who I treated each had babies over a three year period, and all of them were born on the first day of the month. Each of the women was trying for her first baby and was experiencing difficulty conceiving. They had heard of my work and decided to give it a try. I often hear those words when I first meet a new client: "I've tried everything else so I thought I'd give you a go". I just smile. I understand how they must feel the first time; often they have tried every alternative and have come to me as a last resort and with low expectations. I understand their worries and their scepticism about meeting someone like me.

One such woman who came to see me said that it was not about any particular complaint, as there was nothing really wrong. I think she just wanted to see what happens in one of my sessions. I have no problem with that, as I think people need to learn firsthand about what I do. I do not believe in shrouding my gift in mystery. Since she did not have a specific complaint, I did a basic assessment of her energy levels and looked for anything that might require adjustment. After her session, she asked if I had ever helped anyone have a baby. When I said that I had, she asked if I could help her friend; she already had a daughter but wanted another child. However, she had a cyst, which needed to be surgically removed, but the operation would leave her infertile. Without hesitation, I agreed to help but then I realised what I had just done; I had agreed to remove a cyst. As I thought about it, I was convinced that I could do it. The very next day my client's friend rang and made an appointment.

The day of her appointment arrived. I opened the door to find the most beautiful looking woman I had ever seen stood in front of me. She was really nervous, so as normal I made her welcome and we soon settled down for a chat. By the time I got around to giving her healing, I knew that I could help her.

When I put my hands over her abdomen, I could tell that the density covered quite a large area; a growth such as a cyst will affect a much larger area and before I could remove it, I needed to bring it together and make it more compact. Although this increases the density, it stops it from interfering with other organs.

She told me that the cyst was large and was in an awkward place. The amount of heat and the area it covered confirmed this. Even a tiny diseased area can produce a substantial amount of energy and cause significant discomfort in the surrounding area, in this case the entire abdomen. A lot of shearing would be needed to remove the negative energy, and I had to move quickly because her operation was already booked. This was her only chance and if I failed, it would mean she would be unable to have any more children. After her first session, we made an appointment for the following week. I knew that she could be called for her operation at any time, but I had a feeling that everything would work out for the best.

As soon as she arrived for her next visit, I could see from her face that things were much better. She told me that her abdomen felt a lot better and that the swelling had gone down. I repeated what I had done during the first session, trying to take away the energy that was feeding the cyst. At this point I had no idea if I would succeed, because the cyst had a blood supply which had allowed it to grow that large. It was that blood supply I needed to target. I did not want to give her false hope, as I knew the enormity of the task I was facing; here was a young mother with a massive cyst in one of the most delicate areas of a woman's abdomen. If the cyst had to be surgically removed, she would lose any chance of having another child. My guides told me that the body had made this cyst and so I had a chance to take it away. I knew that I had to do my best for this young woman and I tried to reassure myself by focusing on what I would learn.

Something told me that I had to approach this cyst from both above and below so that the energy would flow from both directions. I placed one hand under her back and the other on her front. What a good decision that turned out to be; the heat just exploded. It seemed as if there was enough heat to boil a kettle! Then I started shearing as much as I could so that the heat would not be absorbed back into her body.

When you work on a solid object, you have to make it as hot as possible to start the healing process. The heat does not come from my hands, but from the negative energy manifesting within the illness, and my hands are looking for the heat source. However, if my hands begin to get hot when a client first arrives, it means that their negative energy is deep. I know it's there, but I need to warm the area first to coax the trauma up to the surface.

As I was coming to the end of this lady's second session, my hands had gone purple. I knew when I saw the colour that she had had a powerful session. Purple means communication. Massive communication had been used that day. I needed cold water as it dispels negative energy. Before and after every client I run my hands under the tap. When I had finished her session, I was standing at the sink and I was wondering how the intense heat had affected her. Her eyes were already open when

I walked back into the room. When I asked how she was feeling, she described having experienced several different sensations; she said it was as if all her muscles had been moving at once and then her abdomen would get really warm and then suddenly really cold. She said that she felt completely different and that her abdomen felt empty. I told her that she needed time to come around properly after such an intense session but she insisted that she felt fine. She was able to sit up and after a few minutes, she was ready to stand. Most of my sessions last for an hour but I had worked on this lady for two hours, so I was quite surprised by the speed of her recovery after such an intense session.

If I have the time and I think I can do more, then I prefer to continue and achieve as much as possible. Because she was scheduled for an operation, I could not afford to waste time. We booked her next appointment and off she went. I began to get a very positive feeling about her and her situation. I knew I had a good chance of clearing that cyst. Everything was looking good. There was such a change in her and she felt less swollen and bloated and was much more comfortable. The strain on her face when she first came to see me had lifted, and she looked much happier in herself.

She had a total of seven sessions and by the end of the last one, I felt as if the cyst was gone. Not long after our last session, it was time for her to visit the hospital. I think I was more nervous than she was. I had a massive lump in my throat and felt sick just waiting for her hospital appointment and the scan. This was very important to me; I knew how badly she wanted another child and I wanted to be able to help her.

The day of her hospital appointment finally arrived and I was glad that I had my work to distract me. I knew that I had done my best and that whatever happened was meant to be; perhaps she was not meant to have any more children. About mid-afternoon, she rang and told me that the cyst had gone and the area around her ovaries was completely clear. The operation had been cancelled. I could hardly believe what I was hearing and my eyes started to well up. My face was black with mascara from the river of tears running down my cheeks. I was so glad that I had no more clients that day as I would have found it impossible to concentrate. I felt certain now that she would have the baby she desperately wanted and less than a year later, she gave birth to a healthy boy. She had a perfect pregnancy and a textbook delivery. What a result! I was absolutely delighted for her and her family. God bless.

Most of us assume that when we want to start a family, nature will just take its course, but unfortunately this is not always the case. When couples experience difficulty in conceiving, it can be the most desperate and heartbreaking of times. I know how hard it can be to find the strength to carry on when that longed-for baby remains just a dream. I was first approached to help with infertility early in my healing journey. At that time, I had no idea whether I could help but the experiences detailed here suggest that healing can be beneficial in treating fertility problems.

In 1996, I was contacted by a woman whose fallopian tubes were badly damaged. Both tubes were affected, although in different ways, so I had to treat each tube individually. When I was satisfied that I had done everything that I could, I sent her home and she did not contact me again. Quite some time later, I was invited to a wedding. During the service, I noticed the woman sat on the other side of the aisle, nursing a young baby. I felt it inappropriate to approach her as she had not contacted me since her treatment but it is always rewarding to know that I have helped to bring a new life into the world.

Another client who came to me for help with fertility is Jackie. She has kindly agreed to share her story in her own words:

'We were married in 2000 and shortly afterwards we started trying for a baby but unfortunately nothing happened. I went to see my GP and was referred for IVF treatment in June 2004. This is when the journey started. My first appointment at the IVF clinic was in June 2005. We were told there was a ten month waiting list, but in reality it was a little longer than that. The injections for our first IVF treatment began on 29th August 2007 but sadly the attempt failed in October 2007.

I started seeing Anne in February 2008. She said that all was fine with me and my reproductive system was in good working order. Anne said that she and her boys would sort me out and she could see me with a baby. After each session, I would go back to my husband and tell him all about the experience. He was skeptical, though and thought my visits to Anne were just a way of keeping me happy for the time being.

The injections for our second IVF treatment began on 5th March 2008. Egg collection was carried out on 7th April 2008 and the treatment was stopped half way through. I was told by the clinic that the embryos would be frozen due to suboptimal endometrial growth and evidence of fluid collection in the endometrial cavity. The IVF clinic requested me to have a diagnostic hysteroscopy [a procedure used to view the inside of the uterus by inserting a camera into the uterine cavity, which helps doctors to check for abnormalities and problems in the reproductive tract) and adhesiolysis (a procedure used to remove scar tissue inside the uterus and in the reproductive tract). These procedures had to be completed before they would perform the frozen embryo transfer. Anne would reassure me at our sessions and tell me to be patient and that a baby would happen.

I still continued with the medical professionals and made an appointment with my gynecologist privately on 22nd April 2008, where I was put on a waiting list for the above procedures.

I rang enquiring about my appointment in December 2008 and was told that my notes had been lost. After numerous telephone calls and letter writing, I eventually saw the gynecologist on 31st March 2009 for the procedure. At the appointment I was told by the gynecologist that he couldn't understand why I was there and that I would not be having a procedure carried out on that day. Fortunately, this was because I was pregnant! How amazing! Anne was right! I am not too sure what happened during my sessions with Anne or what she does. All I experienced was seeing colours, feeling a waving sensation in my abdomen and then I would fall asleep. I would wake up feeling happy and for some reason would smile and laugh a lot. It was an amazing feeling.

During my pregnancy I visited Anne regularly. I had a dream pregnancy with no morning sickness. I had a caesarean section at 39 weeks. My perfect little angel arrived weighing 7lb 10oz. How amazing! Our little miracle is now 4 months old and she is amazing. Thank you to Anne and her Boys!'

~~~0~~~

Families are very precious as I learned at an early age. The breakup of my own family was followed by the worst days of my life. One day I will write about it and explain how I gained experience in childcare when I was only a child myself; but today is not that day. For the moment, I would like to focus on my next drawing and why it is so special to me and many of the people who have seen it.

It was after treating one of the women experiencing fertility problems that I decided it was time for my next drawing; I called it 'The Family'. It was something that I had been seeing in my mind for some time and I felt that the time was now right for me to draw it. The picture shows a gathering of people with small children, standing together and looking up at the colourful light coming down from the universe. This incredible light shows us the way when it is our time to depart this life. I think it is quite a moving drawing, which has given a great deal of comfort to those who have seen it because of the children in it. The male and female figures are standing together with small children in front of the adults. This indicates to me that if children pass over at a young age, they are looked after by someone already there, even if they do not yet have family members on the other side.

They will still see familiar faces and surroundings. Children forget about the universe after the age of five but if they go back in the meantime they really will be all right, and this picture shows the most peaceful scene of that event. It looks as if they are looking up to the light waiting for someone to come back. It is a very peaceful drawing and a most beautiful scene. It has plenty of admirers and I am particularly fond of it.

The purpose of this drawing, which shows people together, is to provide answers to the questions that we all wonder about at some time. For example, 'When it is time for us to die, will someone who has gone before come to support us on the journey?' Regardless of our religious beliefs, there is always someone that will come for us when it is our time to leave this life. It is usually a family member or close friend and their presence will bring a feeling of incredible peace and love.

CHAPTER SIX – The Elements

When a new baby enters the world, its energy input is very high and good care is vital. The baby's lifeline - its umbilical cord - feeds it while the baby is inside its mother and this energy flow continues throughout and immediately after birth. For this reason, it is important that the umbilical cord should not be cut until all the blood has entered the baby's body. This process is visible, as blood flow will decrease and the cord will become pale. The baby then has the right amount of fluid and the energy balance is optimised. It is only as the child gets older that the balance starts to tip and this is the beginning of imbalance.

As babies grow, families can sometimes lose interest as the baby becomes harder to control and sleeps less. Children who were picked up often as babies usually want more attention from their parents as they grow up. In families with only one child, this is not normally a problem but in larger families it can be very difficult. Second, third and subsequent children can miss out on a lot of love because parents do not have as much time to spare. As a consequence, these children will often subconsciously seek support from the first child to compensate. Parents often tell younger children to play with their siblings, not realising that the child may not be receiving the right amount of energy from both parents.

Children need the right combination of male and female energy to keep their energy balanced. This is why both parents are so important to children's development. There are usually fewer problems in families that are well balanced. But where the father is away a lot or absent altogether, there are often problems with at least one member of the family. If there are more than two children, it is usually the middle child who is affected. The eldest child may take energy from the middle child without realising it while the middle child is so grateful for the attention that he would do anything that the older child asked. Young children readily absorb the energy around them, just like a sponge and it is terrifying to think that a small child could be absorbing the friction from all the family just by being present. The long term consequences and detrimental effects often do not become apparent until the child is older.

If we look back on our own lives, most of us will have learned some hard lessons. With hindsight, perhaps we could have made life easier for ourselves, but then we would not be the people we are today. We must all learn the hard way, but sometimes we may feel that we are going round in circles, trying to deal with the same problem. This is the time to stop, as we are in danger of stagnating and allowing the vicious circle to continue endlessly.

At this point, I would like to pose a question to each of you individually: how are you feeling and why? If you are anything less than happy and content, you need to take control of the way in which you think, or else your brain will just chatter on endlessly. Try to find peace within yourself.

If you find it impossible to gain control of your mind, I suggest that you try the following exercise. But a word of caution; only do this if you have the help and support of someone you can rely on. I would not recommend facing this process alone as you may stumble over many things that make you feel worse than you did in the beginning, but with the right support, you will get through it.

First, you need to identify and understand where and from what time in your life your unhappiness stems. To do this, you will need to visit the times and places again in your consciousness by first going back through your life. Begin by going back as far as you can remember and make a note of how old you were at each significant event. This will make it is easier for you to establish how old you were when the trauma began. Once you have done that, you should be able to pinpoint what was happening at that time in your life and thus identify the root of the problem.

Please do not underestimate how painful this process can be, but it does help to get rid of the dark side of your thoughts and get your thinking back on track. It can turn out to be a journey of enlightenment. Writing your thoughts down can help enormously as it is a way of taking them from the conscious and is a form of release, which can be calming.

~~~0~~~

I firmly believe that it is important to help my clients understand how and why we get ill. Illness does not just happen: we must be experiencing a trauma of some kind or another for illness to be able to get to us. It can infiltrate us in many ways and can be very destructive. The extent to which illness affects us depends greatly on us as individuals and how well we are able to deal with things that happen to us. If we are mentally strong enough and do not let things intimidate us, we can avoid illness altogether. Some people can go through life unscathed while others have everything thrown at them but they survive. It all depends on your mental state.

To illustrate this, I want to tell you about some of the many cancer patients I have worked with who have struggled with extremely difficult treatments. A patient's mental attitude can affect the way that they cope with their illness and learning to come to terms with the reality of the disease and adopting a positive attitude can have a dramatic effect on the course that an illness takes. Cancer is no different to any other disease in that respect and while it is not always possible to cure cancer, what is important is awareness and acceptance.

The energy that I work with can help us to understand and have awareness that there is more to life than we may first have thought. Fear is usually rooted in a fear of the unknown. There have been many occasions when my work has helped an individual to understand and accept what is happening to them and those people have gone on to survive the illness, but there have also been times when I could not achieve that difference in awareness and acceptance. But even on those occasions, clients have been given an insight into the secrets that the universe holds of the journey that awaits us all. In dealing with cancer, we must not be sad. Please understand that I do not make that statement lightly, for I have lost many of my own family to this dreadful disease and I still ask why it happened.

Our minds have the power to help sustain a more relaxed approach to illness and, if we can accept that illness is caused within us and is related to our lifestyle, it is much easier to understand how the illness developed in the first place. Many people today lead lives that are very hectic and it is widely accepted that stress has a huge impact on our well-being. When we are stressed and tired it is easy for our thought processes to become negative. The majority of people who I see with cancer describe having some form of trauma in their lives within the five years preceding diagnosis and have not yet been able to overcome their emotions in dealing with that trauma.

As individuals, we should not underestimate the effect that our mental attitude and emotions can have on how our physical bodies deal with illness. A person who is relaxed and determined to fight an illness typically responds much better to treatment. Some clients require several sessions before they grasp this and it is only then that they can begin to come to terms with their illness and fight it head on.

Undeniably, people with cancer suffer great mental trauma as a result of their illness and if I am to have any chance of treating the disease, I need to help them to understand the importance of changing the way that they think. Successfully changing our attitude requires commitment, hard work and perseverance, as it is extremely difficult to maintain a positive attitude when those around us doubt that it will make any difference. Most importantly, they have to really believe that it will change things for the better.

In the fifteen years since I began my healing journey, my experience has shown me that the difference between the people who survive cancer (and other diseases) and those who do not always comes back to the same question: do they truly believe that they can overcome the illness? While I fully appreciate and respect the importance and role of conventional medicine, I want to illustrate to you how dramatic the effects of adopting a positive mental attitude can be.

The client who I am about to describe required at least three sessions before he began to adopt the necessary attitude to deal with his illness, but after that the difference soon became apparent. He started to respond extremely well, walking regularly to get more exercise and eating more than he had for months. His whole attitude to his illness was so different and the improvement in him was incredible. He changed completely; his quality of life was so good and his health would improve daily. He did much more than he had for a long time and soon felt able to walk several miles each day. He also decided to go on holiday.

His mental attitude was at an all time high, but all that was about to change. During one of his sessions, he mentioned that he was to have a blood transfusion and when I asked why, he replied that he had been told that he needed it. A recent blood test had shown that his white blood cell count was down, meaning that his immune system was low.

His doctor suggested that he should see his consultant.

At first, the man was not worried because of the quality of life he was enjoying, but the simple act of being told that his blood count was down and that he needed a blood transfusion was enough to bring the illness back to the forefront of his mind. This in turn made him ill as it unbalanced him and his thought pattern that had taken so long to build. How true it is that the thought is the deed and that the way we think is the way we are. Although that man knew that he had cancer, together we had balanced his mind to understand that he was in control of the energy and of the spirit.

In order to fight a disease such as cancer, it is important not to be intimidated by its presence. Yes, it might be in our bodies but the secret of improving our chances of survival is not to let it take control of our minds. We must use our inner strength and the knowledge that we have the ability to fight it. That, in my opinion, is the answer; by keeping our spirit strong we are able to be in control. If we worry constantly about our illnesses, we will worry ourselves into an early grave, but if we are able to take control of how we think, things can turn out very differently.

I do recognise though that it is not always easy and there are few things that remind us of our mortality more than the presence of young children in the family. A particularly good example of this is a client who came to see me because she had lung cancer. I was teaching her to use her own energy to keep her spirits high and she was soon doing so well that she began walking every day.

The difference in her was evident to all around her. Even though she had lung cancer, her mind was focused on living and enjoying her life. Hers was a close family and she saw her grandchildren often. One day it struck her that she might not be around to see them grow up. It was not something that she had really thought about before and the realisation hit her particularly hard. I have not seen her for some time but I understand that she is spending as much time with her family as she can.

I referred earlier to my belief in karma and how we have to put good thoughts out to the universe in order to get good thoughts back. I believe this to be a good philosophy in all areas of our lives and as part of our daily routine. We should all strive to achieve calmness and contentment in our lives as like attracts like. If we can achieve this, we can live our lives in harmony and peace. In order to experience how that feels we need to take better care of ourselves and not worry so much.

As we travel through life, we need to ensure that the direction in which we are headed is right for us and that we are happy most of the time. We are quick to blame others just because things do not turn out as we planned. The mundane chatter in which we sometimes find ourselves engaging indicates that the mind is not at rest. Sleep is vital and waking up tired suggests that the mind is still active while we should be resting both our bodies and our minds. Modern life can be very busy and many of us ask far too much of ourselves. We do not allow enough time and we often give ourselves a list of jobs that is totally unachievable. Our minds are constantly buzzing with noise and information and so the challenge is to close down our minds and enjoy more restful sleep. We can do this by taking time to unwind properly.

Giving our minds commands and taking control takes work and it is important for each of us to find a way that suits us as individuals. Many people find it helpful to practise projection. Begin by finding somewhere that you feel comfortable - it could be an armchair or your bedroom or even your car - and relax. Do this for ten minutes each day for the first week. Next choose a place that is special to you. It should be somewhere you can easily visualise and that gives you a feeling of peace, as this is the view that you are going to use as your focus. As you sit and relax, picture the special place you have chosen and try to recreate how you felt when you were there. Because you have given the brain a command, it will act upon it. Take your time, slow your breathing right down and enjoy the tranquillity. This is your time to give healing to yourself. We are all capable of doing this.

You may find different methods that work for you, for example writing down your thoughts and worries to offload from the consciousness. It simply means you can read them instead of allowing them to constantly occupy your mind. Some people find chatting with friends more of a release, while others prefer to meditate. What is important is that we find an outlet that works for us, a way that allows us to take control of ourselves and to start to understand just how the universe works. That is my passion.

~~~0~~~

The next case that I am going to tell you about still surprises me even now. Dianne has given permission for me to use her real name and I would like to thank her for agreeing to share her experience.

Dianne was one of my oldest and most loyal customers from the salon. She had been unwell for a long time and after many tests she was diagnosed with gallstones. Stones in the gallbladder are not unusual and there are normally several small stones but Dianne's case was different. She was found to have a huge single stone in the gallbladder, which is very unusual.

When Dianne first became ill, she could not eat anything containing fat or cream. She was suffering from severe heartburn and even foods such as milk began to cause her problems. This went on for months before she finally saw her consultant. She was told that she would have to wait at least six months for an operation and so I suggested to Dianne that I may be able to help.

The first thing I wanted to work on was taking away the heartburn that she was suffering from. After about three sessions the heartburn started to improve and Dianne found that she could eat more of her favourite foods again. Before long, the heartburn had nearly gone and she was feeling much better in herself. But something strange was happening. Whenever I was working on her it sounded like all around her gallbladder was popping. It was very loud and happened at each of her healing sessions. We used to laugh about the popping noise every time she came to see me.

After a few more sessions, Dianne looked and felt almost as if nothing was wrong and could eat almost anything she wanted. She brought her sister, Barbara, to one of our sessions so that she could watch what happened. As I started to get closer into the area on which I was working, I could clearly see all the red energy that needed to be removed. But nothing could have prepared me for the shock that I felt when Barbara told me that she could see what I was doing and described it to me, without me saying a word to her. She told me that she could see the area I was working on.

After a few months, I told Dianne that I did not need to see her again. I could no longer see or feel any hot spots and I knew the stone had gone. But we needed confirmation so Dianne went to see her doctor to ask for another scan. She must have been so nervous - can you imagine telling the doctor that a huge gallstone had just disappeared? Unsurprisingly, he did not believe her and thought she was scared of the operation. It was obvious that Dianne was going to have difficulty persuading the doctor to send her for another scan and, with Christmas fast approaching, she decided to wait until the New Year before trying again.

Dianne had a lovely Christmas, eating whatever she wanted, but we only had until February to get the doctor to agree to another scan. Unfortunately you cannot just demand a scan but it was plain to see that she no longer needed an operation. Dianne went to see the doctor again and told him that the gallstone had gone and although he still did not believe her, he was so fed up of her asking for a scan that he finally agreed. I was so excited when I heard, but nervous at the same time as I had even begun to doubt it myself, despite having helped many people with gallstones and kidney stones.

The day of the scan arrived and I was working as usual. Dianne's appointment was in the afternoon and Barbara was going with her. That morning seemed to last forever but finally Dianne rang. The doctor who had performed the first scan had been there and he remembered Dianne as soon as he saw her, again remarking on how unusual it was to see a single large stone. He asked why she wanted another scan but when she said that she thought the stone had gone, he replied that he did not think that was possible due to the size of the stone. Imagine his surprise when the scan showed that the stone really had gone. I was so thrilled when Dianne received the official results of the scan - her doctor could not believe it. Dianne has been fine ever since and has had no further problems.

The next case that I would like to share with you is completely different but no less exciting. This man was a carpet fitter by trade and so much of his work involved kneeling. He had been on sick leave for about eight months with a bad knee and despite having seen many doctors, nothing seemed to be working. Like so many others, it seemed that I was his last resort. When he first came to see me, the man was in agony and could hardly walk. He told me about all the pain he had experienced in his left knee. He was still in a great deal of discomfort and it was obvious that he needed help.

The left side of the body represents the female side and the problem with his knee told me that he was expressing some sort of problem. Our knees carry us through life and they can take a lot of strength. If we have a problem with our knees it indicates that someone or something is quite literally bringing us to our knees. Sometimes we have to bend to the pressures of life. I think there were other problems that were playing a part in this man's life as well and so I wanted to do as much as I could to help him.

At the first visit, I like to establish what is going on and why. Once I know how long the person has been ill, I can tell how long the negativity has been there and how much damage it has done. The body can heal itself but I need to know what is wrong so that I can decide where to start and determine whether or not the problem is structural.

I began by putting my hands around the knee but not touching it. I was looking for heat so that I could determine the amount of negative energy present and its density. I needed to know whether it was loose energy or the glue-type substance that I have mentioned in previous chapters. It turned out to be the latter, which needs to be warmed to get as much heat out as possible before I can start to remove it. The process of warming the energy loosens it sufficiently for me to be able to pull it out. I knew that it was important not to pull too soon as this can damage the tissue, especially since the density of the glue-type energy was likely to be pushing the knee joint out of shape. This was probably causing a lot of the pain, so I knew I had to take my time and let the heat do the work. I hoped that he would feel a lot better when I had finished his first treatment and that his knee would be a lot looser, allowing him to walk more easily. This man had been unwell for eight months, so it was very important to achieve some relief for him.

At the man's second appointment, I looked inside the knee to see if the colour had changed. When energy is circulating correctly, it appears as a golden colour. If I see a colour other than gold, I know that the energy is not reaching the areas it should. Black indicates that the energy is very deep in the body and is not flowing. If there is pink or red in the black then that indicates trauma and means that I need to use the shearing technique to bring the energy to the surface and allow me to see more clearly what I am dealing with. It can sometimes take a couple of sessions for me to be able to get inside of the area to have a better view.

I knew that this was what was needed with this man. Slowly the darkness cleared and I saw what looked like tiny pieces of grit being arranged into a pattern. In my mind I sensed that the pieces of grit would all be brought out through the skin and the feeling was so strong that I actually said it out loud to the man. The way he looked at me suggested that he did not quite know what to say - he probably thought I was mad! I tried to reassure him, telling him that he would probably notice bruising over the top of his knee the next day but that he should not worry. This was only his second visit and I still remember the look of bemusement on his face as he left.

The very next day the phone rang; it was the man's wife. She said that his knee was in a real mess; it was badly bruised and the skin was pitted with little stones. I explained that the grit had to be brought out of the knee and that this should happen the next day. She seemed dubious and I did my best to reassure her, telling her that this was what was supposed to happen. As I put the phone down, I was practically jumping up and down with excitement. All I could think about that evening was how the grit was going to come through the skin. I could not wait for the next day to arrive.

Halfway through the next morning I received a call, telling me what had taken place in the night. When the couple woke up in the morning they noticed that the bed was very wet. Throwing back the covers they found a lot of blood in the bed. On closer examination they saw little black dots in the bed that looked like grit. It was then that they noticed the man's knee; there was a perfect round hole in it. Alarmed by the appearance of his knee and the blood-soaked bed, the man's wife insisted on taking him straight to hospital. When the man was eventually seen by a doctor, the couple described what had happened during the night. The doctor examined the man's knee carefully and asked if he was in any pain. When the man replied that he was not, the doctor said that his knee looked fine and sent him home.

When the man came to me for his next appointment, his wife was with him. They were both still in shock about what had happened to his knee. The man's wife asked if she could have her husband's appointment that day as she had been very depressed for a long time but could not find an obvious reason for it. Depression is much more common than we realise. It affects many people at some point in their lives and can be very debilitating, so I agreed to do whatever I could for her. As she lay on the couch, I got to work. About halfway through the session, I suddenly started coughing violently. I could not breathe - it felt like the air around me was filled with smoke. Somehow I found the breath to say so out loud. The woman jumped up, startled at the mention of smoke, and told me that she knew where it was coming from.

Sometime in the past there had been a fire. The woman had come home from work one day to find their house on fire. A neighbour had called the Fire Brigade but it was too late and the couple's house had burned down. She told me of the trauma she and her husband had suffered and how they had both dealt with it in their own way. It seemed to me that this was the root cause of both their problems. The woman had suffered from depression and the man had been brought quite literally to his knees by the combined trauma of the house fire and his wife's depression.

I have not seen them since that last appointment but I hope that the help I was able to give them has changed their lives for the better. God bless them both.

This next client has come a long way from the time when I first met her over seven years ago. Denise had become very ill after complications following on from breast cancer and had been in bed for a long time. She had been in constant pain and was confined to her bedroom for much of the time. It was a friend of Denise that told her about my work and suggested that she should see me. That is how all my clients come to me - via word of mouth. Previous clients have passed my name onto friends and family and I firmly believe that the people I see are meant to come to me.

It must have been very traumatic for Denise to visit me as she so rarely left her own home. She was so unwell that even the doctors made home visits. Nevertheless, she was determined to see me. When she arrived, she was bent over double and obviously in agony. I was almost afraid to even touch her but I knew that I had to do whatever I could to make her better.

Clients normally lie down for their healing sessions but Denise's physical movement was very limited and extremely painful due to her having been lying on her back for months after surgery, so I asked her to sit on the couch instead. When she was seated, she began to tell me her story. It was difficult to comprehend just how long Denise had been suffering. After many failed attempts at reconstructive surgery, she had all but given up on leading a normal life. For years the pain had been so excruciating that she could hardly move and she had endured many hours of physiotherapy to try to regain some sort of movement in her back. But nothing had worked; it was almost as if she had seized up and was finding it difficult even to stand for any length of time. Then, out of the blue, someone told her about me.

At Denise's first appointment my boys wasted no time at all in getting to work on her and although I have seen this many times, it never fails to amaze me. It is just incredible to watch. The boys treat each client as an individual and so everyone's experience is different; the movements and the power applied are sometimes so extreme that the client's physical body is almost tilted! The movement is sometimes so intense even in elderly clients that at times I wonder how the human body can take this sort of pressure but I have learnt that the boys do whatever the body needs. But Denise just took it, even though her body had not moved like this for years. I knew that she must have been in a lot of pain at times and I was glad when her first appointment came to an end because I hated to think that my boys and I might be causing her even more pain.

But the boys were not content to finish there and they continued to work on Denise at home when she was relaxing. Suddenly they would start to move her in the same way as in the healing room. She recalls several occasions when she was sitting in her living room and her arms suddenly began to move. She would have to lie down or straighten herself out so they could work on her. Slowly, she began to really respond to this treatment and the difference in her after a couple months was startling.

I know how difficult it must be to visualise the boys moving someone's body but on one particular occasion I think they must have decided to show off, because they began working on Denise when her family was at home. It was the longest and hardest session that she had ever had - I think it lasted about three hours – and neither Denise nor her family had any idea what she was going to be put through. It started off as usual but this time a lot of new movements were introduced. Her husband was so amazed that he decided to record what was happening using the video camera. The next time that the physiotherapist visited, Denise told her about her sessions with me and about what the boys had been doing. She offered to show her the video as she had known her for such a long time.

Denise made coffee and they sat to watch the video. I cannot even begin to imagine how the physiotherapist must have felt watching one of her patients being moved into positions that she knew she could not achieve herself. When the video had finished, the physiotherapist asked Denise how she had known about the movements she had seen as some of them were movements that she herself had devised. Imagine the irony of the boys performing movements that the physiotherapist had devised - and on one of her own patients at that!

Denise's recovery of her physical movement has been incredible and she can even dance now, although I have forbidden her from dancing the twist as that seems to upset her equilibrium and cause problems. The video is still safe and despite many invitations, I have not yet seen it. Perhaps one day I will want to when the time is right.

I was sitting at home one evening just as dusk was approaching. I was thinking of the powerful energy that I was working with when I suddenly had an urge to open the back door. The colours I saw were breathtaking! I could feel the energy, pure energy staring back at me. I went and got my paper and charcoals and the sixth drawing was in front of me. I worked quickly so that I could capture the view. It was almost as if the sky had stopped moving and was suspended in time. While I was drawing, I felt a stronger connection with the atmosphere. The universe is such an unknown entity. The energies are in constant flux, continually changing. I believe it's a reflection on how we live our lives.

Many countries are in decline at this present time, which can be a worry to us all. However, if we can make changes in ourselves then that would in turn make a difference and can bring about positive changes in our lives. I believe we can make a massive difference by being more considerate of our environment and everyone on the planet. We have more influence over how we live our lives than we first thought. I have come to realise that as we evolve it is us who are making the problems that affect our lives so it is up to us to turn it around. Once we understand this and resolve the way we think we can have the lives we want, we will then be able to secure a safer world for our children to inherit.

CHAPTER SEVEN – The Map

In the early days of my work I used to wonder just how long it was all going to last, and if one day it would disappear as quickly as it had arrived. I loved and enjoyed being taught all these new techniques and how quickly it was becoming a normal part of my life. I had a new way of thinking, a new outlook on life. I was changing and growing in confidence and so was my work. The next two chapters explain in detail some of the different types of people that have had treatment with me, the ailments and obstacles that were overcome and the new methods and techniques I learnt. All of this was so frightening and unreal to begin with but is now a part of my everyday working life.

From the very beginning of my healing experience I have always looked for confirmation and someone to corroborate that the healing was real and worked. I know this sounds a bit uncertain but I still couldn't quite get it into my head that this was all really happening, that it was real! There was a particular lady, a regular that came to the salon. I would often think that she needed healing. I was thinking about her one day when she walked in with her husband and Honey the dog. Her husband and the dog would sit patiently while the lady's hair was being done. Honey would watch everything that was going on. There was a reason I was particularly interested in this lady, it was because her foot was black with gangrene!

This lovely couple were waiting for it to get better so they could go away on their boat. I knew that gangrene wouldn't get better. The foot looked as if she had a black sock on, and whenever they came into the salon I could not take my eyes off it. I would always look to see what was happening with her foot and how she was coping. This day she came in and said out of the blue, "OK, OK! I'll let you have a look! I've watched you for weeks now checking me out and I know you've been itching to get your hands on it, so I'll make an appointment". I was over the moon! We made the appointment for the following Thursday afternoon. It so happened that on that day Leslie, a nurse who was also a regular, was having her hair done. As she was about to leave she asked me if I was working upstairs that day. Being a nurse she was always very interested in the work I was doing and wanted to know what I was working on.

I smiled as I said gangrene. "Sorry, what did you say? I did not quite get that". "Gangrene on a lady's foot today," I replied. "You are joking aren't you?" she said. I laughed and replied, "No, I have been waiting to be asked as I have wanted to do this for a long time". Leslie asked if it would be possible to stay and watch. I was not sure about this as confidentiality is of the utmost importance to me, so I said I'd have to ask the lady, who it turned out was agreeable. The lady arrived for her appointment with her dog who went everywhere with her and her husband who never leaves her side. The room I used to do my healing in was very small so I had to make room for everyone.

How we all fitted into the small space I don't know! The lady was on the couch, her husband sat with the dog at his feet and Leslie stood with me at the foot of the bed. Leslie wanted a birds-eye view of what was going to happen. As I said, I had wanted to work on this foot for a long time and it got that I could hardly suppress the urge. I asked how the lady was feeling as I made my preparations. I put my hands over the lady's foot and all of a sudden I stopped. I felt I had to check her arms and legs and look for any black spots! I'm thinking black spots? Ok. After a thorough check I was satisfied there wasn't any, and asked the boys, "Why black spots?" They said it was to be sure the infection was not in the blood stream or had gone deeper into the body. I found when looking at the gangrene that it was as if I was looking right through her foot seeing if there was any life within the darkness. There was not, no sign of normality such as blood vessels or redness of skin and Leslie also corroborated this.

The foot was very swollen, like the swelling which happens when you have a trauma or a bump. It's the body's way of moving the energy outwards and away. Better out than in as the saying goes! My first thought was to get the swelling down, so I began the shearing method moving the energy down through the foot and off the toes. I did this for some time and watched as the foot started to go down. It was as if someone had pulled the plug out of the foot. Each time I did the shearing method the foot would go cold, very cold as if it had been in the freezer! Then I held my hands over the foot to warm it back up again.

This was going to take a while and each time I did the shearing method I pulled the negative energy out of the foot, making a gap in the swelling.

Every time I warmed the foot up it got even hotter than before. Negative energy can only be removed from the body when it is warm or hot. It always amazes me the amount of heat that comes from the area being worked on. As the swelling went down everyone could see the difference. The session went on for more than two hours and shades of pink were now clearly visible through the skin. Leslie could not believe what she was witnessing. She bent down closer to the foot so as to examine the foot herself. The shades of pink were now visible to both of us which meant the blood supply was starting to come back into the foot.

The swelling had gone down so much, I was really happy for the lady. I then had a sudden thought and could hear a voice telling me that the lady was going to be very ill and there wasn't anything that we could do about that. I knew I had to warn her and I really didn't want to frighten her, but she needed to know, I felt awful. I began by telling her that the gangrene was very deep within her foot. "What we have done today is to make it possible to get this infection out and stop it spreading. However, to do this it will make you ill! But you will get better". I was relieved to see the lady took this information in her stride. Next I was being told that I was to create a draining system so the infection could drain out of the foot.

I did not see the lady after that day because she was ill in bed! I was later told that when she woke up the morning after the session she found an abscess on her second toe. This was what was used as a drain until all the gangrene infection had left her leg. The foot had been saved from amputation but sadly this lovely lady suffered a lot of pain because she never came back to me until the foot had recovered completely. If only she had trusted me to continue helping her she would have had no pain at all.

I received a phone call from someone I knew who was concerned about a friend of the family. The man concerned had been ill for some time, suffering from an enlarged heart. I accepted the challenge straight away and made the appointment. Charlie was an extremely sick man; he could hardly stand and was also having a lot of difficulty breathing. This was due to an enlarged heart and major arteries that were blocked. Charlie started to explain to me what was wrong and for how long he had been ill. This gave me an insight into the problems I needed to deal with in the first session.

As Charlie got on the couch I said, "Right let's have a look at what is going on". That's when out of the blue I heard, "Left leg first, nowhere near the heart". I'm thinking, what nowhere near the heart? OK, but why? Then I heard, "Because the arteries are blocked and the blood will have nowhere to go". Oh my God I thought, of course it would make him worse if I'd gone near his heart! I understood what I was being told and was amazed with the information and guidance that was being directed toward me. Charlie soon settled down and rested while I began to give him healing on his left leg, he was very weak and grey in colour.

I just couldn't stop thinking of how the instructions came to me, it was amazing and I just knew this healing was going to improve Charlie's life. I was now on a mission and was determined that this first visit was going to be the start of a new lease of life for him. I worked away unblocking the arteries in the left leg. Charlie could feel everything as I worked on him. He looked as if he was shivering and I recognised that as a sign of the nerves reacting to the energy coming in and the unblocking of the meridian lines. This is also described by some clients as a vibration throughout the body, which helps bring balance throughout the system.

Charlie's colour started to improve rapidly in such a short time and he was so pleased that he had come to see me and the boys. After that first session was over I watched Charlie leave and thought to myself how he looked like a totally different person compared to the person who had knocked my door! I couldn't wait to see him again the following week. It was all so new and I loved my work and all the new challenges I was experiencing. I felt very blessed and humbled to have been trusted with such a considerable responsibility. I was on a path and had no choice but to carry on as I feel people's lives and their well-being are things we cannot take for granted. I feel truly privileged to be chosen and guided to help others in this way.

All week I thought of Charlie and I had this overwhelming feeling that he was going to recover and get his life back on track. When Charlie arrived for his appointment he looked just as good as when he had left my house the week before. This was so encouraging. As Charlie took off his shoes I left the room to wash my hands and when I came back he was already on the couch. I smiled as that is always a good sign. We chatted until I was ready to work. This time it was his right leg that needed to be unblocked, almost the same as with the left leg except that it was more intense because the right leg contains the main artery to the heart. Charlie commented on feeling things moving inside him. He said he could feel a rush go through him right up to his torso and chest. As the session progressed I realized I needed more time with Charlie. I needed to finish the job properly and hopefully bring his heart back to normal size and working condition.

The end of the session was here before I knew it. Charlie looked so comfortable I didn't disturb him and went out and washed my hands leaving him for a while.

Later as he sat putting his shoes on he told me how much stronger the healing session felt. I explained that we were moving closer to the heart and that's why it felt a lot stronger. Anyway I said, "You are looking so much better". He agreed that he did and more importantly felt better, so an appointment was made for the following week. I knew this next visit was going to be something different. I was looking forward to it all week as I could feel his energy had shifted.

When Charlie arrived he told me he had received a letter from his consultant totally out of the blue! An appointment had been made for him for a routine checkup. He said he went to the hospital at the appointed time and date but when he arrived he was told he was not expected? They agreed to see him and found that all his arteries were unblocked and the blood was flowing freely. I was delighted with the news; however, I realized we were not out of the woods yet. I knew this was a delicate part of his healing and had to turn my attention to the heart as we needed to get it back to its normal size.

Charlie got on to the couch ready for the session. I suddenly felt unsure and thought to myself, this is the man's heart! I calmed myself as I knew I was being guided and what had to be done. I sat to the left of him and did as I was instructed. I worked from the hip up towards the chest and heart. The heart is the pump and I needed to work towards it and hopefully reduce the size.   I had not experienced anything like this before and had to trust my instincts and be guided. I was slowly moving my hands across Charlie's chest when I felt a massive amount of density that is the only way I can describe what negative energy feels like to me.

Negative energy, especially when it's been there for a long time, has a funny sort of feeling, like a glue-type substance and before I can move it, I have to warm it very gently from the outside in. This must be done slowly as the heart is the major organ in the body. Charlie said he could feel his muscles in his chest moving so I explained this is normal, it's the torso relaxing after being restricted for such a long time. Of course this felt very strange to him so I kept reassuring him all was ok. Charlie told me what he was feeling so that I could understand exactly what was happening.

This was a fantastic lesson for me and showed me so much in a short time. They were teaching me to understand the body not in medical terms but in healing terms. The body was reacting to the negative energy being released and healing energy being put in. While I was working on him I felt an urge to put my hands in and pull out all the negativity. I didn't because it was the heart and I knew I had to work slowly, in a very careful manner. I could tell the session was coming to an end as my hands were extremely hot and needed to cool down.

I left Charlie to rest for a while as he'd had another very strong session. I knew he needed another session like this one and decided to give him a two hour session on his next visit. I needed to finish off getting the negative energy away from the heart, thus reducing it back to its normal size. Charlie's next visit came around quickly and he was looking so different compared to the first time I met him. He looked 10 years younger and much healthier in all ways! I was close to finishing Charlie's treatment and was as excited as he was with his improved health. In total Charlie received seven hours of healing with me and we both felt it had been a huge success,

In the following weeks Charlie was examined by his consultant who confirmed that all his arteries were working and unblocked and that his heart had gone back to its normal size. This really confounded Charlie's consultant as to how he had recovered and he kept asking Charlie lots of different questions. It was Charlie's choice not to disclose any details of the healing he'd received to the consultant as he thought he would be laughed at and not believed. I have not seen Charlie since but have heard he is doing fine.

I met John through his sister Irene who was also a client who'd had treatment with me. The first time I met John I was shocked; I had never seen anyone so grey! He was having great difficulty with breathing as he had been suffering from emphysema and had been like this for many years. John was looking after not only his dear wife but her mother and his daughter who was suffering from M.E. I was amazed that this man was able to do so much considering how ill he was himself. Life with emphysema is a struggle. Just to do everyday tasks becomes extremely difficult because of breathing problems. People that suffer with this need to have oxygen close by at all times and the lungs fill with fluid which if not drained can over time drown a person.

John wasn't a young man and I felt I needed to sit and think about this as I had not attempted anything like it before. In the back of my mind I knew this one was a tall order but was willing to give it a go. I explained this to John and he replied, "What have I got to lose Anne? Have a go you might learn something new, you never know until you try". John's attitude was wonderful and I knew I had to do what I could. The first appointment arrived and I suddenly became aware of what to do. The heat in his chest confirmed to me the seriousness of his illness. I let my hands search for the most congested areas, finding out where the hot spots were. I checked everything thoroughly so that I knew exactly what I was dealing with.

Into my mind came a blueprint, that's the only way to describe it. This was for me to look over everything and get a clear picture of what was needed to be done and where to start with John. As John started to relax I could tell he was absolutely exhausted. He said he could happily stay on the couch all night and he never moved a finger for the whole session. It is quite surprising how many people comment on how comfortable the couch is, and how they don't want the session to end. After a session I always make sure my clients are all right to drive and with John it took him a good twenty minutes before I felt happy for him to drive home.

Once the first session was over I knew how I would approach this ailment. John and his family realized how much work was needed to bring this illness under control so they all pulled together and helped one another with their daily tasks. John was there for everyone in his family and did so much, so I made sure on each visit he was given absolute priority. By the second session I was ready for John and was instructed to start with the sides under the arms. I have to do exactly the same on each side such as shearing ten times from the right and the same on the left. This is vital to keep the balance in both lungs.

John could feel the pulling straight away. I didn't pull too much for the first session as I didn't want to make the lungs sore. There was a lot of fluid in the lungs and I wasn't sure just how it was going to come out. The fluid had been there for a long time so I was being very careful with my approach, until I was shown just how this was going to affect the area. I was really happy with the progress that was being made in this session. When John opened his eyes he said, "I want to make another appointment for next week". I started giggling I couldn't help it. "Oh Anne, this is doing me so much good, I can tell the difference already".

I was always ready and waiting for John to arrive. The techniques I was being shown were new and exciting. I didn't want to waste any time and it was vital that I did my very best. John was using three types of pumps throughout the day to help him breathe. He didn't sleep well and was propped up by loads of pillows during the night. Imagine how uncomfortable it must have been not being able to lie down to sleep. It was on our third session. I was sitting on John's left side when I suddenly noticed a tray to my right. I couldn't believe what I was seeing as it appeared from nowhere.

On the tray were what looked like medical instruments. I sat there trying to figure out how to get the fluid out of John's chest. That's when I noticed huge tubes on the tray that looked like syringes, and then everything clicked into place. I realised that I was being shown what to do! I knew I had to get this right so I calmed myself before I began. I was being told to go through the motions of removing the fluid with the injection type instruments, but instead of giving an injection, I would take it away by drawing it out. As I started to push the invisible needle into John I asked him to let me know what he could feel. John told me he could feel a pressure of something going through his skin. At this point I was not touching John at all. John could feel the invisible needle going into his side. Once the needle was in position I could start to draw out the fluid by visualising the tube filling up.

While I was working there was a light coming from the floor. It was just indescribable, and the ambiance in the room took on a new dimension. I realised I was not alone, that I was being taught a new skill. I kept doing the same action time after time until the session was over. When I looked at John his colour had dramatically improved and his breathing had become more stable. Week after week John would come for his treatment and the change in him was phenomenal. John was sleeping much better as he no longer needed so many pillows. The amount of medication he was taking had reduced by more than half. However, this was only for a short period of time as it soon became apparent that John no longer needed to take any medication at all! John is living a very happy healthy life and is doing well.

Audrey had heard about me from a friend and, taking the plunge as she later told me, picked up the phone to make an appointment. Audrey lived in Barry about 5 miles from me so not very far to travel. I found Audrey to be a very jolly person and we hit it off straight away. I loved listening to her as she was always busy organizing some sort of event. Audrey loved meeting up with her friends a few times a week for dancing. Dancing was a big part of her life so when she became unwell with her hip, it really affected her quality of life.

The day of Audrey's first appointment arrived. Once Audrey was settled on the couch I found the heat coming from her left hip pretty nasty. I concentrated on using the shearing technique to remove the heat. Then Audrey started telling me about her heart problems and pending operation. It came to light that Audrey was waiting to go into hospital for a heart bypass and valve repair. I suggested that I could give the heart some treatment after working on the hip, not realizing the impact I was going to make. After a few sessions Audrey was delighted with the improvement in her hip. It was about this time she received her hospital appointment.

Audrey came to see me for a final treatment just before her operation. She was a bit nervous but her spirits were high. The session was more reassurance than healing and as we said our goodbyes she told me that she would ring me to let me know how the operation went. My thoughts were with her on a daily basis in the hope that we would have a good result. Audrey phoned me a few weeks later and told me the exciting news; everything had gone really well, and to the surgeons' amazement the bypass no longer needed to be done, just the valve repair. Audrey was absolutely delighted with the result and her recovery went from strength to strength.

Pat and Brian kindly gave me permission to use their real names while writing this next account. This is a heart warming story of a lovely lady's fight with one of the most destructive and common illnesses affecting people today. Cancer has been around for many years and sadly we all know someone who has suffered from this despicable disease. Even the word cancer can and will strike terror into our hearts and many still think of cancer as a death sentence. Just the thought of being diagnosed with cancer and the painful treatments and suffering that go with it is far too much for most people to even contemplate.

This is very sad as we are not giving ourselves a chance, and it does not have to be this way. Today there is a lot of progress being made in this field, and many cures and positive results are being discovered. However, some people will still think 'this is the end'! These people will truly believe there is no cure and so just give in to the disease without putting up a fight. This is such a shame because fear has them tightly in its grip, and they give up because they think there is no hope. Four years ago Pat, an extremely brave lady, was diagnosed with cancer and from the very beginning she was determined she was not going to give in to the disease.

It was the 1st September 2006 when I received a phone call from Audrey telling me she had recommended me to her friends Brian and Pat. Pat had been very ill in hospital with cancer. Then Brian phoned me and briefly explained what was wrong with his wife. I listened intently as he slowly told me everything that had happened. I could hear the pain as he spoke and knew he felt he was at his wit's end. Pat was in hospital and had been there for over six months suffering from a most crippling form of cancer diagnosed as Non-

Hodgkin's Lymphoma; this is cancer of the drainage system.

Brian sounded so desperate it really pulled on my heart strings and I felt I had to give this a go as there might be a chance I could help her. Brian said they needed help as they felt they were running out of time. Pat had lost a lot of weight through this illness; she only weighed 5 stone and was becoming extremely weak. After talking things over Pat and Brian decided it was time to leave the hospital and come home. I was shocked at their decision to leave the hospital but they felt it was for the best. I was determined to do all I could to help such a lovely couple and such a very brave lady.

Pat and Brian arrived for their first appointment on time and as they walked into my healing room I couldn't take my eyes off Pat, she was this tiny little lady and so very, very frail. I thought to myself, have I bitten off more than I can chew? I knew it was in me to try anything, and with the help and guidance of the boys we would give it our all. As we sat down Pat and Brian went into detail about the time that was spent in hospital, and all the treatments given to her. I listened intently, and wondered how I was going to approach this crippling illness that had pushed this lovely couple to the limit. I wanted to end the suffering this brave lady had been going though.

Pat had been lying in hospital for 6 months with so many people trying to help her and nothing had worked. As she was sat in front of me I knew that I had to start behind the ears and down towards the neck. Pat was skin and bone, it was horrendous to see, and the poor darling had been through so much, I really felt for her. As I held and looked her over I slowly went through her body so I could feel exactly what the body had been through. I could see her lungs were full of fluid and it was difficult for her to breathe. I knew I had to unblock the drainage system before I started on the lungs, so I started at the neck and under the arms.

Certain areas of her body felt very lumpy as is to be expected with this condition; by unblocking the drainage system the fluid can leave the body in a more natural way. The first session came to an end and I was pleased with what had been achieved. We sat and chatted for a while and it was then I learned that Pat and her husband Brian had made up their minds not to go back to the hospital. They asked me if I could help Pat and I said, "Yes, I feel I can". That was the start of an amazing journey for us all. I realized this was going to test my work to the highest level, and I also knew I was going to help get rid of this horrendous cancer.

I just knew there had to be a way around this terrible disease and was determined to find it. Pat's consultant was going to monitor her throughout the time she was having healing with me. We all knew this was not going to take just a couple of sessions, but we were all very positive knowing the hard work involved. A huge task of combined effort was required, and as long as we all worked together we knew a difference would be made. I have come to realize that to change something we have to set goals.

I was looking forward to seeing Brian and Pat again and as their appointment got closer I started to home in on Pat and trusted the feelings I was receiving on how, where and what I was going to be doing on each visit. It was necessary for Pat to be seen twice a week, simply because of the amount of work that was needed. This also had to be done as quickly as possible so as to settle the body down after suffering six months of hell.

The body had been through a huge amount of trauma and needed to be calmed down. By calming and settling the body it has a better chance of reacting quickly to the healing energy. If negative energy has been present in the body for a long period of time it is like trying to remove glue. Negative energy thickens over time so when healing takes place this energy has to be softened. By softening it makes it easier to move the unwanted energy away from any of the vital organs. This gives the organs room to stretch back into their correct positions and allows them to function properly, thus starting the healing process.

The next visit came around quickly and as Pat and Brian walked into my healing room I could see she was busting to tell me something? Pat had put on a pound in weight! I was as delighted as they were. Pat then told me her tummy felt tight. I said, "Your stomach muscles need loosening that's what the boys are telling me". I gave Pat breathing exercises to help the loosening of the stomach muscles. This in turn would encourage everything else to loosen. It felt like her torso was in a vice, a huge block of negative energy.

The lungs were a big concern to me because of the build up of fluid. Pat was still in great pain due to the body being so tight and because of previous procedures where they had tried to remove the fluid from the lungs. Pat commented on how many lumps she could feel in her groin as we were discussing how we would approach draining this area. I started to use the shearing method on the lungs and Pat started improving on every level. I then put Pat into the colours. This is a form of secondary healing but at a universal level. It means every colour that is produced has the most powerful healing effect on the mind and the body. What happens in the mind happens in the body. When using this method the results are astounding.

When clients are in this dimension the state of consciousness is at its highest with regard to universal energy. Changes on a huge scale can be achieved and sustained and this healing energy will continue at home. People would recognise this as a form of meditation without consciously preparing to go into a meditation. The universal energy will recognise when the body is relaxed, and therefore be able to connect. This state of consciousness enables the healing process to continue, allowing clients to stay within this consciousness at all times. This is difficult for some people to understand, but it can be achieved. The energy level has to be built up within the body so it has something to work with and can be sustained.

Many people who have received healing from me have experienced continuous healing throughout the rest of the day and night. In some cases this has carried on until their next visit and all have benefited greatly from this. While Pat was receiving healing, her husband Brian would also be in the room. After each session he would also look much better. The universal energy was good for them both. Pat was due to have her fortnightly visit at the hospital. This was only the second week I'd been seeing her, but the lumps had disappeared from her neck and arms and her weight had increased by one pound. I knew we had a long way to go and couldn't wait to see how the hospital would react to the changes in Pat's condition.

When Pat arrived for her next treatment I could see they were both upbeat and in a positive mood. Pat had put on yet another pound in weight. I was so delighted, as a pound a week would make such a difference to her. Next I had to concentrate on

Pat's lungs as she had had a drain inserted for over six months while she'd been in hospital. As I worked I started to reduce as much fluid as possible. I used the same method I used when treating emphysema. I have only experienced this once before with a client called John, who has had no problems since he came to me. Pat's husband Brian would be present throughout when I used my secret methods. This made me feel nervous, as I was not ready for anyone to see how things were done as I was only just getting used to it myself.

I have not told anyone of how I'm being taught or my secret methods on how fluid is removed from the lungs. I explained to Brian that all my methods are confidential and I didn't want him to tell anyone about what he saw. I explained that some of my methods may seem a bit quirky but they do work! Brian understood completely and said, "I don't mind how you do it as long as it continues to help Pat improve". Having the medical world keeping a close eye on things also put our minds at rest. I sat on the side of the lung that Pat said was the most uncomfortable.

As I prepared to work with Pat my tray appeared in full view on my right hand side. On this tray were all the implements I needed to do this particular job. The fluid had to be taken out of the lung and the most favourable place was under the arm above the waist. I gently felt for Pat's ribs and that gave me the indication for the gap between the ribs so that I could insert the invisible tube. I dared not think of how all this was happening and I know to most people this sounds ridiculous, impossible and other worldly. All I can say is that the way I work is not of the world as we know it, but many surgical treatments have been done this way with great success.

I used exactly the same method on each lung. Brian could see all my hand movements which indicated the fluid was being drawn out of the lungs. I had not done this type of work with a third party present before but Brian wanted to be with his wife at all times. When this method of treatment is complete I sit behind the client with my hand on their shoulders, which sends energy down through the body to the feet. The client will experience warmth and tingling sensations which in turn confirms to me that the meridian lines are unblocking.

These methods have to be repeated over and over again until all the fluids in the lungs are removed. Brian commented on how Pat's quality of life was improving on a week to week basis.

Every two weeks Pat went to hospital for an x-ray to check on the fluid in her lungs. As each month went by Pat couldn't believe how well she felt and looked. Brian was so overwhelmed by it all but he didn't want to say very much; I think he didn't want to count his chickens before they'd hatched. Pat's doctor could see for himself that something was working, but all he would say was I don't know who or what is making you better but something is! One hospital appointment in particular caused everyone to sit up and take notice. The doctor brought up all of Pat's x-ray's and showed her how the fluid in her lungs had decreased on every visit until they were completely clear. On the 6th September 2011 it will be five years from the day that Pat arrived at my door. Everything in Pat's life is back to normal and she is living her life to the full. God bless them for having the courage to try something different and having faith in me and the boys.

~~~0~~~

The time had come to do the seventh drawing. The drawing depicts a planet I don't know what this represents. It is like looking at a map with an island at the top. Why a map I just don't know. I understand the need for my other drawings and the energy they are directing. I really don't understand this one at all or what benefit it has to do with my work! I had put all my drawings up on the wall in my healing room but with this seventh drawing I decided to hide it behind the door where no one could see it! The reason I hid the drawing is because I thought it was absolutely hideous and I really don't know why that is. I have not shown the drawing to anyone. However, it has been noticed occasionally when the door was closed. I have always been so proud of all the other drawings and I feel frustrated because I don't know why I don't feel the same way about this one.

CHAPTER EIGHT – The Circle

I have certain clients who have had very close physical handling with the boys, and find that they are being moved in the most unimaginable way! June came for healing and was lying on the couch while the boys vigorously worked on her. She was being tilted up onto her side, and was so close to the edge that I wondered if she was going to stay there! With that, she was encouraged off the couch and onto the floor. I found this all very fascinating, especially the expression and expectation on her face. As June left the comfort of the couch and moved onto the floor, she had a look of pure determination, as if no-one was going to stop her from doing this! The energy being used was physically powerful, a determined no-nonsense flow that was a unique remedy for her particular problem.

The move to the floor happened because more room was needed so the boys could get to work on June without any hindrance. They would stretch her into all sorts of positions, positions that I'd never seen before and that looked humanly impossible. The base of the couch would also be used as leverage when exercising her legs. One at a time her legs would be lifted and moved about in exactly in the same way. June took this all in her stride; the boys knew exactly how much pressure to apply when working on her. It was astounding to watch her body being pushed and pulled into these different and unusual positions.

June originally came to me for leg and back problems and a few minor things that we all get from time to time. When someone is having healing I never know what exactly is going to take place as it depends on the individual. Over the years I have got used to the unexpected! June wanted her husband to come and observe, as he would not believe her when she told him what she was experiencing. June's meridian lines needed to be reconnected so this particular way of healing was a bit different to say the least! Most of my clients stay on the couch to have treatment, but for June it was not the case. She brought her husband with her to her next appointment. He was quite hesitant and unsure as he could not find an explanation for what his wife said was happening when she visited me. He just could not believe any of this was possible.

We started the session and he watched as the boys worked their magic. He was shocked and said to his wife, "Well, I've never seen you do anything like this before!" June replied, "That's why I wanted you here, so you could witness what happens when I have healing!" I interjected and explained to her husband that the stretching he was observing was to strengthen her limbs. He joked that he thought her legs looked longer after a session with me! This was how he dealt with what he was seeing, as he could not explain it. Over time the benefits of having such a powerful treatment were plain for all to see. The improvement in June's overall wellbeing was so apparent that she eventually felt she didn't need to see me on a regular basis. It is not always necessary for people to come for healing continually. Many come because they feel down or they want a top up, or may even just fancy a session.

Stewart's visits were not the same as most people's and over time he has built up a special relationship with the boys. I don't know of anyone else who has the same rapport with them as he does, and his treatment reflects this. Every time Stewart arrives for his session it's all pretty normal to begin with. Then as I prepare to give him healing that's when small movements are noticed, as if someone is playing games. Stewart's sessions are fun and the level of interest that the boys show in him and their playful antics indicate that they have a sense of humour, and a special bond has been formed. Stewart has a gentle nature, similar to the feeling I get from my work. I don't know why they have taken to him this way or if there is a reason for it.

Stewart first came to me because of a problem with his right elbow. He had been suffering for some time, and he couldn't straighten his arm. He had been to the doctors but nothing seemed to help. In the beginning the thought of coming to see a healer and not knowing what lay in store intrigued him, and he found it a bit of a novelty. Stewart's first session lasted a few hours. As I gave him healing he described what he was feeling and how strong it felt. I explained there was a lot to do, as this problem had been there a long time.

The boys were telling me that the elbow had to be made bad before it could be made better. I had not been doing surgery for long and was still a bit uncertain of what could be achieved. I needed the feedback from my clients and Stewart was happy to oblige. I was soon to realise how much more I was going to learn due to his elbow being an on-going problem. Throughout I was taught and guided by the boys. They explained that something in Stewart's life had not been resolved! He was bending to accommodate a male energy, but it was negative energy. This was ongoing and his elbow would not heal until he dealt with whatever was affecting him. When we get reoccurring health problems there is always a worldly problem related to it.

In this case the elbow indicated not bending to life's problems. Another example is, say, a problem occurring in the shoulders. It means someone is leaning on you. The right side of the body represents male energy and the left represents female energy. Depending on which side the problem is, will tell if it's male or female related. Stewart had put his problem down to long hours driving without rest. He would also keep his arm in the same position for long periods of time. As this was Stewart's first session it took a bit longer; he had been on the couch for over two hours. I had run overtime, and knew I had another appointment due.

While working on Stewart I noticed it had started to get dark outside, so I bent over to the small table near the couch, and put the lamp on. The blinds were almost closed and at that time I didn't realise people could see into the room from the outside. Unbeknownst to me, my next appointment had arrived. Kate sat outside in her car while she waited for me to finish what I was doing. Her car was parked right next to the window of my healing room. Kate could see me working near the couch and noticed a little girl dancing around the room. As Kate waited, she saw me leave the room and knew I had finished work so she knocked the door. I opened the door and offered her a seat while I went to wash my hands. This is very important and has to be done before and after each session.

As I walked back to the healing room I said to Kate, "I won't be long". "OK," she replied. Walking into the room I noticed Stewart was lifting his hand up. It looked as if he was going to shake someone's hand. I looked at him and said, "I think they are going shake your hand, have you been talking to the boys?" He replied, "Yes I just thanked them for making my arm better," and with that the boys shook his hand! I had never seen anything like it, I was bowled over! I asked Stewart if he minded me opening the door so Kate could observe the contact being made. "Yes," he said, "No problem". I opened the door and it felt as if we were very much as one at that moment; we all had tears in our eyes.

As Stewart left I led Kate into the healing room. She looked at me in confusion and asked, "Where's the little girl, Anne?" I said, "What little girl are you talking about? There isn't any little girl in the room there's only been Stewart". As I settled Kate onto the couch she insisted that there was a little girl. She had watched her dance around the couch and pass by the window. Kate described the child to me: "She's a pretty little girl, Anne, with long blonde hair and she was wearing a white dress". I didn't know what to make of this but Kate was adamant that she had clearly seen the little girl while sitting in her car! After our chat we settled down to her healing session, but I could not get it out of my mind. Kate was in no doubt about what she had seen. The session ended and Kate left. I went out to the kitchen to make a cuppa and think about all the things that had happened that evening.

There was a knock on the door. It was my friend Mandy, who was also one of the girls from the salon. Mandy has seen many things to do with healing. In the early days when my healing gift was just beginning, Mandy would sit in while I worked and confirm that she had seen the same things I had. "Come in Mand, I've got the kettle on," I said. I was so pleased to see her and began to tell her everything that had happened that evening. As I started to tell her about the little girl she gasped, and put her hand up to her mouth. "Oh my God!" she said, "I saw her in the room". I never said another word while Mandy explained exactly what she had seen.

It transpired that Mandy was walking passed my flat to go to the phone box directly across the road. "Anne, I always look over at your house just to see if your lights are on in the healing room, that's how I know if you're working or not and if it's ok to call in. That's when I saw a little girl dancing around by the window". Mandy also said the little girl was wearing white and had long blonde hair. Well, imagine what my face must have looked like,

I could not believe it! I wanted to go into the healing room all the time after that just to see if I could spot her, or see her as I see the boys. I didn't see her, but just knowing she is there gives me a lovely feeling.

As Stewart's healing sessions continued the boys became more playful with him. I laugh whenever I think of the time they would not let him leave the room. As Stewart got off the couch the boys started to pull him onto the floor! It looked as if he was being jumped on and by the time they had finished with him the state of his clothes looked as if he had slept in them. When he did manage to get up off the floor he tried to make his way toward my desk so he could make another appointment.

He would giggle with embarrassment, bright red in colour, walking as if he was drunk. It was one of the funniest sights I have seen. They would immobilize his hands to stop him from getting his wallet out! We would both be in tears of laughter. As Stewart tried to walk he found he had no coordination, he was totally unable to do anything about this and it happened every time he was leaving! This would go on for ages and by the time he left Stewart would be in a right state, but he loved it. He really enjoyed the playful antics and thought his visits were fantastic.

On another occasion, Stewart sat on the settee to take his shoes off. I was preparing the couch when I turned around and stared as Stewart was being held by both ankles and being pulled off the settee. Stewart was desperately trying to hold on to the arm of the settee as they pulled at his legs, trying to wrestle him to the floor. He was holding on for dear life and giggling his head off, but the boys won and Stewart ended up on the floor. Every time he tried to get up the boys jumped all over him and wrestled him back down! Stewart could not stop laughing and it was absolutely hilarious to watch. I would stand there with tears rolling down my face saying, "Stewart, will you leave those Boys alone!" Between his laughter he replied, "Anne, it's not me, it's them!"

I loved the way the boys played about with Stewart as much as he did. In one session they brought his arms above his head, cupped his hands together and did a perfect golf swing. He was being shown techniques on improving his golf! Another time as he was putting his shoes on they buckled his fingers so he couldn't tie his laces! It was as if to say "You're not going anywhere yet, we're still playing". Whenever Stewart made an appointment I would make sure we had plenty of time just in case we needed it, because we never knew what they would do to him next! I have never seen the boys play this way with anyone else. It makes me laugh when I imagine opening the door to my next client with Stewart, a grown man, lying on the floor, being jumped on by some invisible force, unable to get up and laughing himself silly! The look on their faces is priceless.

I loved my healing room and was being asked by the boys to draw on the wall. I didn't want to spoil my lovely healing room by drawing on the wall! I was thinking, for goodness sake! What are they thinking of? I was digging my heels in because I didn't want to draw on my wall. I thought it would look hideous and stupid putting a drawing onto the wall! However, I felt compelled to do just that. I was being directed to draw a huge circle in the middle of my wall. It was Easter bank holiday and I kept seeing lengths of string, like shoelaces. The boys were insistent and showed me exactly what they wanted. I kept thinking that I needed to get the right paint to do the job, hoping I could stall them. Then loud and clear I heard, "You already have the paint, a gold spray in a tin, it's under the kitchen sink!"

I knew then that I could not put it off anymore. I walked into my healing room and looked at the wall. It was the largest wall in the room. I moved the settee out of the way and stood back and thought, 'How am I going to reach up to the top?' I thought, 'This is so stupid, I really don't want to do this, it's a Sunday morning for goodness sake and I should still be in bed having a rest!' Lengths of string kept coming into my mind, it was then I took a lace from one of my trainers, got the gold paint, that I didn't realise I had, and got my charcoals ready. I used the lace to draw the outline of an enormous circle and did this by tying one end of the lace to a pencil. Holding the other end, I found the centre point of the wall. Inside the large circle I drew a smaller circle by folding the lace in half. In the middle was a triangle and at the centre of the triangle was an eye.

The gold paint was used to outline the large circle and a thin layer of blue was used on the inside. The small circle and the triangle were drawn in gold. Around the circle I put these little shapes; the only way I can describe them is that there is a similarity to the pattern on rune stones. These shapes had to be in perfect precision, and spaced out correctly. I was then directed by the boys to put a gold spot on the right hand side of the circle. To explain where I put the spot just for a moment, imagine the circle was a clock. The spot was positioned between the hour and quarter past the hour. The positioning of the spot was very important and it was imperative I got it right. The spot had to be in alignment with the centre point of the inner circle. The drawing took me two and a half days to complete and the bizarre thing about it was that the phone never rang and nobody called, which is most unusual.

After the bank holiday I started back to work. My first appointment was with a new client. I opened the door to two ladies; I realised my client had brought her friend for support. A lot of people bring a friend or family member when they first come to me as they don't know what to expect. My client's friend sat on the chair by the window opposite the wall where the circle was. I was busy giving healing to my client. As the session got underway I noticed her friend looking towards the wall. I thought to myself, 'I bet she is thinking what on earth has she done to her wall?' I was a bit embarrassed and was waiting for her to say something. Here it comes I thought. The lady said, "I've seen that drawing before". "Pardon?" I replied in astonishment. "That drawing on your wall, it's similar to one in one of my books; next time we come I'll bring it with me". I was absolutely stunned and wondered whatever next.

My client's friend kept to her word and brought the book on their next visit. The book was titled 'Lost Civilisation of Mu'. I had never seen this book before and wasn't sure what I was going to see, but she was right. It was a drawing of the inner circle with the triangle and the eye in the centre. The circle or shield (as the book described it) was also edged with shapes similar to those I'd drawn, but only a few shapes. The lady said she wanted me to keep the book. After that occasion many people that came for healing would say they thought the drawing was a shield hanging on the wall and not a drawing at all!

I had no idea that the universe held so many secrets or that I was so ignorant to it all. I always thought of myself as just a mum and hairdresser, even a bit of a workaholic as some friends of mine would say! I enjoy working and have been lucky to have met some lovely people and made some great friends along the way. I have always been a very caring person and have helped out many people and their families throughout my life. When I was a child I looked after lots of children. I was babysitting when I was still a child myself. As with most people there have been times when things didn't go well for me and I had to make certain decisions. I look back and think I wish I had never done this or that, but don't we all, and at the time whatever I did I thought it was for the best.

Today my life has changed beyond all recognition compared to how it was. Everything has changed from the way I think to the way I live since I began this journey. I was so sceptical in the beginning, I kept thinking 'They're going to come and take me away because none of this is real. It's all a crazy dream and I just wanted to wake up!' What I didn't realise back then was that I was just starting to wake up to a reality that I had never known was possible or even existed.

When I look at my life at this point in time I realise how far I have come and how much I have learnt and am still learning. There is so much I want to share with everyone but I realise people need to make their own minds up; that is the reason I wrote this book.

I am used as a channel for the healing energy to come through, and during a session my thoughts become one with the universe and the powers that be.

The universe is a part of every one of us. We are connected, and always have been. My clients are from all walks of life and different backgrounds. The boys are from another dimension within our universe. They have shown their commitment time and time again and proved that we are all connected. On many occasions my clients describe the energy they feel as being like waves of vibration going through their bodies. This vibration I believe to be the connection to the magnetic field which surrounds us all. We can all take ourselves to a different dimension when we daydream or meditate; this is also a form of self hypnosis. It is a way the mind can rest and re-charge whether we realise it or not.

Never underestimate the power of the universe, and the connection we all have with it.

The elements can change at any time, as we know.